The Rapture Verdict

Michael Snyder

-CONTENTS-

-CHAPTER ONE-

Why Write This Book?

Why in the world would anyone want to write this book? The timing of the rapture is one of the most hotly debated topics in the Christian world today, and one of the fastest ways to get other believers to turn on you is to take a strong stand on this issue. By writing this book, I am likely going to upset many of my readers, some of my oldest friends and even members of my own family. So why bother to write it in the first place if it is just going to create problems for myself?

Well, the truth is that what we believe about the second coming of Jesus Christ really matters. It is mentioned approximately 300 times in the New Testament, which breaks down to about once every 25 verses. If God did not want us to study these things, there would not be such a vast amount of material in the Bible about the last days. God clearly wants us to understand what is going to happen, and any Christian leader that is purposely avoiding this topic is doing a great disservice to those under his or her care.

And whether we want to admit it or not, what we believe about the second coming of Jesus makes a significant difference in how all of us are living our lives on a daily basis right now. In this book I am going to explain how bad teaching about the rapture is causing a tremendous amount of damage to the body of Christ. There are millions upon millions of believers that are making absolutely no preparations for the hard years that are ahead of us because they are absolutely convinced that we are going to be pulled out of here before anything really bad happens. And there are millions upon millions of believers that are in danger of totally missing out on the incredible plans that God has for them because they are so focused on the "imminent rapture" that they think could happen at any moment. Great challenges and amazing opportunities lie ahead, yet so many Christians have completely given up on life and are just counting down the days to their one-way flight home.

Unfortunately, there isn't going to be a pre-Tribulation rapture. In fact, millions of Christians are going to die waiting for a pre-Tribulation rapture that is never going to happen.

This is not an easy thing to say, but someone has got to be willing to stand up and tell the truth.

Someone needs to clearly and accurately explain to the people what the Bible really says about the return of our Lord.

Someone needs to be courageous enough to step up and take all of the abuse that is going to come from those that have extremely deep emotional investments in the idea of a pre-Tribulation rapture.

There is so much confusion and dissension regarding the second coming of our Lord and Savior, but this should not be the case. If you don't take scriptures out of context or try to twist them to fit your own pet theories, the Bible is actually exceedingly clear about what is going to happen. My hope is that this book will bring a tremendous amount of clarity to this debate that has been missing up to this point in time.

According to the Pew Research Center, 48 percent of all Christians in the United States believe that the second coming of Jesus Christ is going to happen within the next 40 years. That means that there are tens of millions of people in the U.S. alone that believe that they will see Jesus return within their lifetimes. And if Jesus is on the verge of coming back, that has dramatic implications for every man, woman and child on the entire planet. The Bible tells us that the most chaotic period of time in all of human history will be right before the return of our Lord, but most evangelical Christians in America have become convinced that they aren't going to have to face any of it.

For the past several decades, evangelical churches in the western world have overwhelmingly taught that the rapture comes before the seven year Tribulation period, and therefore believers will get to escape all of the chaos described in the book of Revelation. In this book, I am going to show that this theory is not true at all. Throughout the New Testament, there is one Greek word that constantly shows up in passages regarding the second coming of Jesus Christ. That word is "parousia", and it can be translated as "coming", "arrival", "presence" or "official visit". As you will see, multiple scriptures tell us that the rapture will happen at the "coming" ("parousia") of Christ, and the New Testament also makes it clear that this "coming" ("parousia") will come immediately after the end of the seven year Tribulation period.

The seven year Tribulation period is also known as "Daniel's 70th week" and "the Time of Jacob's Trouble", and in this book I will show that it comes to an end when the 7th trumpet is blown in Revelation 11. That is when the rapture takes place, and it begins a period of time known as "the Millennial reign", "the last day" and "the Day of the Lord".

In Joel 2, the coming of the Day of the Lord is described as a time "of darkness and of gloominess, a day of clouds and of thick darkness". It is during this transitional period of time that the vial judgments will be poured out, and the fall festivals of Rosh Hashanah, Yom Kippur and the Feast of Tabernacles provide a template for the events that will take place during this stretch.

In the end, the Antichrist will be totally defeated, and the Lord Jesus Christ will reign from Jerusalem over the whole planet for 1000 years. For those of us that are believers, we very much look forward to that time, but for now there are tremendous challenges immediately ahead of us. Jesus is coming back for a bride without spot or wrinkle, and the trials and tribulations that we will face during the coming years will purify and refine us.

In this book I intend to very clearly lay out the truth, but I hope to do so in a spirit of love. No matter what my brothers and sisters in Christ may believe about the timing of the rapture, I choose to love them as family, and hopefully those that wish to engage me on this issue will take the same approach. As you read through this book, you will notice that I never tear anyone down or attack anyone personally. Yes, I do address doctrines that I believe that are false very directly, and that is necessary because these doctrines are doing an immense amount of damage to the body of Christ. But at the end of the day this is an inter-family debate, and it should be treated as such. Those of us that belong to Jesus Christ are going to spend eternity with one another, and our Savior wants us to learn how to love. May we all grow in love even as we debate emotional issues such as this one.

Without a doubt, the timing of the rapture needs to be addressed in an honest way. In America today, we have gotten to the point where many churches completely avoid any discussion of the rapture altogether. And it is easy to understand why they do this. If you offend some of those that are listening to you, that is going to lead to smaller crowds and smaller offerings. And needless to say, those are things that some ministries want to avoid at all costs.

Other ministers are constrained by those that they are accountable to. For example, if you are a pastor of a mainline denominational church and you want to change your perspective on the chronology of the last days, it could end up costing you your career. Many denominations and churches require strict adherence to their particular doctrinal positions, and those positions are hammered into those that are being trained for ministry in their seminaries. So don't expect an honest or independent opinion on the rapture from the pastor of your local church. In many instances, they are simply going to tell you what they have been trained to tell you.

In this day and age, it is absolutely imperative that we all learn to think for ourselves. If you allow someone else to do your thinking for you, it could result in some absolutely tragic mistakes. In fact, I know quite a few people that have actually made major life decisions based on end times theories that the "experts" taught them.

Well, I have personally met a number of these so-called "experts", and the truth is that they do not deserve to be put up on pedestals. Many of them are grossly twisting scripture, and you may be surprised to hear that a lot of what passes for "Bible prophecy teaching" these days is simply made up out of thin air.

When we exalt the traditions and doctrines of men to the same level as the Word of God, we are bound to get into big trouble. No matter who is telling you something, and no matter how good it may sound, if it does not line up with the Word of God it is not to be trusted.

As an attorney, I was trained to be skeptical, and I was taught to only come to conclusions that are warranted by the evidence. In this book, I am not going to try to make the scriptures fit into some preconceived doctrinal agenda. Instead, I am simply going to lay out what the Bible very clearly teaches.

In 1837, a fairy tale entitled "The Emperor's New Clothes" was published by Hans Christian Andersen. In his story, two tricksters convince an emperor that they have made him a set of clothes that is not visible to anyone that is stupid or incompetent. So when the emperor starts parading around in his new "outfit", everyone is afraid to point out the obvious because they don't want to be considered stupid or incompetent. Finally, a little child blurts out that the emperor "isn't wearing anything at all" and that is what brings the ridiculous charade to an end.

Similarly, in this book I am going to point out the obvious. In the case of the pre-Tribulation rapture, the "emperor" definitely doesn't have any clothes on, and it is absolutely critical that the church wakes up because this doctrine is hurting millions upon millions of people.

You see, the truth is that there is not a single passage in the entire Bible that clearly says that there will be a pre-Tribulation rapture. You can search until the cows come home, and you will not find one.

Instead, what you will discover is that the Bible very clearly teaches that Jesus is coming back immediately after the Tribulation. This has been the majority position all throughout church history, and in many areas around the world it is still the majority view today.

I think that it is important to confess that my view on the timing of the rapture has changed dramatically over the years. When I was growing up, I fully trusted what my parents taught me about the rapture, and they fully trusted when they had been taught by the "experts". As I got older, there were always certain passages in the Bible that troubled me, but I ignored them because I figured that the "experts" knew much better than I did.

That was a tragic mistake, and thankfully I learned to think a lot more critically in the years ahead.

As you will see in this book, the most popular theories regarding the timing of the rapture in the Christian world today have no scriptural support. But many believers have very deep emotional attachments to what they have been taught regarding the last days, and so if you start chipping away at their cherished theories it can provoke some extremely strong negative reactions.

I know that there are some people that will be exceedingly upset at me for the things that I am about to share, and I know that I will probably lose some readers by publishing this book. But that is okay. Unlike most ministries these days, I am not attempting to maximize attendance or donations. I am simply trying to please my Lord and Savior.

I do not represent any particular church, denomination or ministry, and I am not going to try to convince you to believe some theory that someone else wants you to embrace. Instead, I am going to attempt to let the scriptures speak for themselves. Because ultimately it doesn't matter what I think, what you think, or what the "experts" think. In the end, the only thing that matters is what God has told us through His Word.

Sadly, most people end up believing exactly what they want to believe. So if you want to believe that some particular theory about the rapture is true, the evidence that I am about to present will probably fall on deaf ears.

But if you are truly a seeker of truth, I believe that you will find what I am about to present to be very persuasive.

We are all learning, and things will become clearer for all of us as we draw nearer to the return of Jesus. I know that my own personal views on Bible prophecy have shifted tremendously over the past 30 years or so. So it is in a spirit of humility that I submit my findings to you in this book.

As you begin reading, there are a couple of things that I want to warn you about. First of all, I quote an enormous amount of scripture, and in many instances I do so in very large blocks. This book truly is a "Bible study" in every sense of the word, and way too often Christian leaders are guilty of pulling verses totally out of context in order to try to prove a point. Even though my large blocks of Biblical text are going to increase printing costs, I believe that giving the reader a sense of context is absolutely critical.

Secondly, there is quite a bit of repetition in this book. Normally, this is something that I try very hard to avoid in my writing. However, in this case it is exceedingly important to understand how all of the pieces of the Biblical puzzle fit together, and in order to do that I found that I needed to come back to certain passages over and over again. By the time you have finished this book, I think that you will understand why.

Thirdly, all of the pieces of this book fit together very carefully like a puzzle. If you only skim through a few chapters, you are only going to get a partial view of the overall picture. Each individual chapter is powerful, but once you complete the book and you stand back and consider the vast mountain of evidence that I have compiled, I truly believe that it will be extremely difficult for anyone to continue to hold on to a pre-Trib or a mid-Trib position.

Whether you agree with me or not, hopefully you will have a much clearer understanding of what the Bible actually has to say about the second coming of Jesus Christ by the time that you are done reading The Rapture Verdict. I want to be fair to all sides of the debate, and more than anything else I want to be true to the Word of God.

Without a doubt, we all need to learn how to love one another and how to have grace for one another. No matter what you may believe about the rapture, I am willing to have fellowship with all of my brothers and sisters in the Lord. Far too often I have seen fellow believers rip each other to shreds over these things, and that should not be happening.

Right now the world is coming against us in thousands of different ways, but instead of learning to love one another and standing together to fight, many Christians are turning their guns on one another. There are billions of souls that still need to hear the good news of the cross, and yet a lot of believers are so busy fighting other believers that they don't have much time for anything else.

If you don't agree with me after reading this book, that is okay. What is far more important is that we learn to love one another. My wife and I are constantly asking the Lord to make us into people of great love, and without great love none of us are going to make it through what is coming in the years ahead.

And that is one of the reasons why I am writing this book. I love my brothers and sisters in Christ, and millions of them have been led astray by some very bad teaching. This is my attempt to correct some of that bad teaching and to get the church to understand what is directly in front of us.

In Matthew 24, the Lord Jesus tells us that the time that we are approaching will be worse than anything the world has ever seen before, and that there will never be a time like it ever again.

God wants us to know what is coming so that we will not live in fear. As I will discuss later on in this book, God is going to be moving even in the midst of all the chaos and darkness. The greatest move of God and the greatest harvest of souls that the world has ever seen are coming, and this is going to be the finest hour for the church of the living God. We are going to be more than conquerors through Jesus Christ our Lord, and the things that God is going to do through us during the years ahead are going to shock the entire world.

Yes, we are going to go through the Tribulation period. But that is not bad news. Jesus is coming back for a bride that is wildly and madly and passionately in love with Him, and the trials that are to come will refine and purify us.

You were born for such a time as this. If you have been searching for meaning and purpose in life, this is going to be a great book for you. It is when times are the darkest that the greatest heroes are needed, and the Remnant is going to provide light and hope to a world that is literally coming apart at the seams.

As darkness rises, we will never back away, back down or back off. Clothed in the armor of God and armed with the shield of faith, we will shatter the enemy with the Word of

God. On our own we can do nothing, but with God all things are possible.

We stand at the most climactic moment in human history, and billions of souls hang in the balance. There are more people alive today than ever before in all of human history, and darkness is rising all around us.

But instead of running and hiding from the darkness, we are going to rise up and be the generation that finally gets things right. The final chapter of the church is going to be the greatest chapter. We are going to bring vast multitudes into the kingdom right here at the very end, and we are going to see the Holy Spirit move in ways that we never even imagined were possible.

You may choose to curse the darkness as it envelops the planet, but I am going to light a candle. Our Lord and Savior has called us to be His bride, and He deserves the very best. The lukewarm, half-hearted religion that passes for "Christianity" in so many of our churches today is not going to cut it anymore. Revival is coming, and it starts with repentance.

We all need to repent for losing our first love. Our Lord Jesus deserves a bride that is absolutely consumed with love for Him. We are called to prepare the way for His return, and so we need to throw off the sin that so easily entangles and the pleasures of this world that so easily take our eyes off of Him.

The hard times that are coming are going to cause millions of Christians to plunge into depression and despair – especially after they realize that the pre-Tribulation rapture that they were promised is not coming. But that is not what God wants. He put us here for a reason, and He has a mission for us to accomplish. I am fully convinced that this is the greatest time to be alive in all of human history, and my wife and I believe that the greatest chapters of our entire lives are still ahead of us.

If you ever wanted to live in "Biblical times", you are about to get your wish. We are going to win vast multitudes for the Lord, we are going to do miracles that are even beyond what we read about in the book of Acts, and we are about to embark on an adventure that is beyond anything that the craziest Hollywood screenwriters ever dreamed up.

So don't look ahead with fear. Yes, all of our lives are about to change dramatically. Death, violence and chaos will be all around us, but we are going to keep our eyes fixed on the author and finisher of our faith. We will overcome the enemy by the blood of the Lamb and by the word of our testimony, and we will lay down our lives for the one who first loved us even if it ultimately means death. We are not afraid, because we know that the day will soon come when the last trumpet will sound and the dead will rise and we will be gathered home. When that day arrives, we will never be separated from our Beloved ever again.

Those that have read the end of the book know that we win in the end. And as each sign in the book of Revelation unfolds, we will know that the return of our Lord is drawing ever closer. When the sky finally does crack open and He appears in the clouds, He will find us building His kingdom even up to the very end.

Thank you for joining me on this journey. I bring a message of hope, and I believe that you are going to be extremely blessed by the things that I have to share. May the Lord

Jesus Christ open all of our eyes as we seek after Him with everything that we have inside of us.

-CHAPTER TWO-

It Isn't That Complicated

Have you noticed that many Christians have extremely intense emotional attachments to their particular theories about the timing of the rapture? Over the years, I have seen people jump through all sorts of mental hoops and twist Scripture in absolutely horrible ways in desperate attempts to defend those theories. But of course very few of those theories even comes close to lining up with what the Bible actually tells us.

The truth is that what the Bible has to say about the rapture is not that complicated if you simply allow it to speak for itself. The word "rapture" is actually never used in the Word of God, but I believe that it is a useful term. When most people use the word "rapture", what they are really referring to is the resurrection of believers that is spoken of all throughout the Bible. The Scriptures tell us that Jesus will come on the clouds with great power and great glory, a mighty trumpet will sound, and dead believers all over the world will be bodily resurrected. At that same time, those of us that are still alive will be suddenly transformed and will meet the Lord in the air.

Nearly all Bible-believing Christians agree that the rapture is coming. It is the exact timing of that rapture where there is disagreement.

Most Christians in America today have been taught that the second coming of Jesus Christ is divided into two stages. Those that believe in a pre-Tribulation rapture are convinced that the rapture takes place just before the seven year Tribulation period, and then seven years later the "Glorious Appearing" where Jesus returns, defeats the Antichrist, and sets up his Millennial kingdom comes at the end of the Tribulation period.

But nowhere in the Bible do we find a seven year gap being taught. On page 69 of his book "No Fear Of The Storm", Dr. Tim LaHaye makes the following stunning confession...

*"One objection to the pre-Tribulation Rapture is that no one passage of Scripture teaches the two aspects of His Second Coming separated by the Tribulation. **This is true**."*

In this chapter, I am just going to give you a brief overview of where we are heading in the rest of the book. Each of the points that I mention here will be examined in greater detail in future chapters. So don't be frustrated by the lack of detail in this chapter. This is just a basic roadmap, and the "meat" of this book will come in the hundreds of pages that follow.

In Revelation chapter 20, we are told that the "first resurrection" includes those that did not worship the beast or his image and that did not receive his mark on their foreheads or their hands. So how in the world can those saints be included in the "first resurrection" if it happens before the Tribulation or at the halfway point of it?

That simply would not make any sense.

In this book I am going to show that there is a single mass resurrection of believers, and that the Bible is very clear about the timing of this event. In Matthew chapter 24, Jesus goes into a tremendous amount of detail about the events of the Tribulation period, and then He tells us that "immediately after the tribulation of those days" the resurrection will take place. You can find similar passages where Jesus explains these things in Mark 13 and Luke 21.

There are times in the gospels when Jesus speaks in parables, and many of the things that He said in that manner can be difficult to understand. Even to this day, sometimes I still come across passages that have me scratching my head.

But there are other times when He was exceedingly clear about what He was seeking to communicate, and Matthew 24 is one of those examples. We will take a much closer look at Matthew 24 in future chapters, but for the moment I want you to pay special attention to what Jesus said in verses 29 to 31...

*29 **Immediately after the tribulation** of those days shall the sun be darkened, and the moon shall not give her light, and the stars shall fall from heaven, and the powers of the heavens shall be shaken:*

30 And then shall appear the sign of the Son of man in heaven: and then shall all the tribes of the earth mourn, and they shall see the Son of man coming in the clouds of heaven with power and great glory.

31 And he shall send his angels with a great sound of a trumpet, and they shall gather together his elect from the four winds, from one end of heaven to the other.

Jesus had just gotten done talking about all of the horrible things that were going to happen during the seven year Tribulation period, and then He tells us that He will be coming to get us "immediately after the tribulation of those days".

I honestly don't see how anyone could misunderstand what He was saying there.

The Bible is not that complicated, and God is not trying to trick us.

If people want to know when the rapture will take place, all they have to do is turn to Matthew 24:29 and read where Jesus said that it will happen "immediately after the Tribulation".

Unfortunately, a lot of people don't have that kind of simple faith. They don't want to believe what the Bible very clearly tells us, and they want to argue about all of the finer points regarding the last days that we find all throughout Scripture.

Well, in this book we are going to look at all of those passages, and we are going to dissect all of the most common arguments that people use to try to explain away the very clear teaching of Jesus.

In the New Testament, there is one Greek word that is more associated with the return of Jesus Christ than any other. It is the Greek word "parousia", and it can be translated as "coming", "arrival", "presence" or "official visit". As you will see in this book, we are told that the rapture happens at the "parousia" of Jesus in 1 Thessalonians 4, 1 Corinthians 15, Matthew 24 and 2 Thessalonians 2. The reason why the exact same Greek word is used in all of those instances is because they are all describing the exact same event – the gathering of the saints immediately after the Tribulation period has ended.

In addition, there are all sorts of other parallels between passages that describe the rapture in the New Testament. In Matthew 24, 1 Thessalonians 4 and Revelation 14 we are told that Jesus comes in the clouds, and in Matthew 24, 1 Thessalonians 4 and 1 Corinthians 15 we are told that a great trumpet is blown when God's people are supernaturally gathered. In 1 Corinthians 15, we are specifically told that this will happen at "the last trumpet". In this book, I will show that this corresponds with the 7th trumpet in the book of Revelation.

Most Christians today do not believe that we can find a detailed description of the rapture in the book of Revelation, but this is simply not true. Because of their bad doctrine, they have simply been looking in the wrong place. When the last trumpet is blown in Revelation 11, we are told that it is "the time of the dead, that they should be judged" and that it is the time when Jesus will reward those that belong to Him. We are also told that this is the time when our Messiah begins to reign. If you look closely at Revelation 11, you will see that it appears to mark the end of one period of time and the beginning of another. I believe that the announcement in Revelation 11 represents the end of the seven year Tribulation period, which is also known as "Daniel's 70th week" and "the time of Jacob's trouble". As soon as that seven year period ends, we begin the Millennial reign, which is also referred to as "the last day" and "the Day of the Lord" in the Scriptures. As I will discuss later in this book, the extremely chaotic period that comes at the beginning of "the Day of the Lord" is essentially a brief transition period between the end of the Tribulation and the great era of peace that our planet will experience when Jesus reigns from Jerusalem. During this very violent transition, the vial judgments will be poured out, Jesus will return with His army, and the Antichrist will be completely defeated.

Following Revelation 11, we find that Revelation 12 and 13 contain side visions, and then the chronological narrative picks up again in the following chapter. And then we find an actual physical description of the rapture itself right there in Revelation chapter 14, exactly where it should be. We find it described after the seventh trumpet is sounded but before the first of the vial judgments is poured out.

In this book, I am also going to discuss how the Biblical feast days that take place in the fall provide a template for the events that immediately follow the Tribulation. Just as the spring feasts were "dress rehearsals" for the crucifixion, death, burial and resurrection of our Savior, so the fall feasts are also prophetically foreshadowing precisely what will happen during His second coming.

For example, I am convinced that "the last trumpet" will be blown on Rosh Hashanah (the Feast of Trumpets) on the day after the end of the Tribulation period during some future year. In this book I will explain precisely why I believe this to be the case.

Following the last trumpet, in Revelation chapter 15 we see a vast body of believers gathered around the throne of God giving Him praise. This group of believers includes those "that had gotten the victory over the beast, and over his image, and over his mark, and over the number of his name". It is very interesting to note that from this point forward there are no more mentions of believers on the earth until we return with Jesus in Revelation chapter 19.

In Revelation chapter 16, the seven vials of God's wrath are poured out. Once upon a time, I believed that this would happen over a period of months or years. But if you actually read Revelation 16, these judgments come in rapid fire succession, and none of them require an extended period of time.

Personally, I have become convinced that these judgments are poured out during "the Days of Awe" which come between the time we are raptured on Rosh Hashanah (the Feast of Trumpets) and when we victoriously return with our Lord and Savior to set up His kingdom on Yom Kippur (the

Day of Atonement). This return on Yom Kippur is described in vivid detail in Revelation 19, Joel 2 and other places throughout Scripture. In fact, if you look at Matthew 24:29 in many versions of the Bible, you will notice that there is a little footnote pointing you to Joel 2:10. Joel chapter 2 is an extended description of the coming of the Day of the Lord, and in Matthew 24 Jesus is indicating that this is the exact period of time during which the rapture will take place.

I know that I have just thrown a lot of detail at you. If you are not familiar with the Biblical calendar and God's prophetic feasts, don't worry, because I will be going into an extended explanation later on in this book.

For now, I just want to give you a broad outline of where we are heading. As this book unfolds, we are going to look at all of the major passages in the Bible that have to do with the rapture, and we are going to dissect the arguments that people use to support various theories about the timing of the rapture that are not Biblical.

The vast majority of Christians in America today believe in a pre-Tribulation rapture. As a result, they are not preparing mentally, emotionally, physically or spiritually for the things that are coming. Nor are they getting excited about the absolutely amazing things that God is going to do even in the midst of all the chaos and darkness. Instead, many of them have already totally checked out on life and are just waiting for their helicopter ride out of here before anything really bad happens.

I personally know quite a few people that have made incredibly important life decisions based on a rock solid conviction that there will be a pre-Tribulation rapture. Perhaps you have family members or friends that fall into the same category. Well, I intend for this to be the kind of book that you can give to someone that needs a big time wake up call.

The church is not going to avoid the Tribulation.

The church is going through the Tribulation.

And I am not just talking about a portion of it – I am talking about all of it.

But don't worry. God knew about all of this in advance, and He has a plan. God is raising up His Remnant, and there will be a place for His Remnant to go. These are things that I will also be breaking down in great detail in this book.

This world is heading for a great shaking. Everything that can be shaken will be shaken, and I am very thankful for that, because without great shaking there would not be great repentance.

For years, God has been sending warnings and sounding a call to repentance all over the world. But here in the United States, hearts are incredibly hard and most churches are either asleep or completely dead. Grace and mercy have not worked, and so now we will see shaking.

As the shaking comes, there will be many that wake up. I believe that the greatest worldwide harvest of souls in all of history will be between right now and the return of our Lord and Savior Jesus Christ, and I believe that the greatest move of God that the world has ever experienced is coming. My wife and I are constantly praying that God would allow us to be part of this. Even though we may know what is coming, there is no guarantee that any of us will automatically get to participate. We all need to press in and seek God like never before so that He can use us in the work that is ahead.

Yes, some incredibly challenging times are coming to this earth. But now is not the time to go dig a hole and try to hide from the world. Rather, now is the time to rise up and to be the people that God always intended for us to be.

We are going to write the end of the story, and I don't know about you, but my wife and I plan to be right there on the front lines leading the charge.

Unfortunately, I find that I have a really hard time getting many believers excited about what God is about to do because they are just sitting around waiting to get raptured out of here. The pre-Tribulation rapture doctrine has produced a lot of laziness and slothfulness among God's people, and it is time that we address this error head on.

It doesn't matter what your opinion is. What matters is what the Word of God actually has to say. And the Word of God simply does not support a pre-Tribulation rapture. You can search the Bible from now until Jesus returns, and you will not find a single passage that tells us that the rapture comes before the Tribulation.

So instead of sitting around waiting for a pre-Tribulation rapture that is never going to happen, now is the time to move forward and embrace our God-given destinies.

The most challenging times that any of us have ever known are right on the horizon, but so are opportunities to do things for the Lord that most of us never dreamed were possible.

Have you ever daydreamed about living during the time of Jesus or during the book of Acts? Well, the truth is that I would rather be living today. We are about to see the book of Revelation come to life right in front of our eyes, and you were created for such a time as this.

It is when times are the darkest that the greatest heroes are needed. If you look back throughout history, the people that you admire most almost certainly arose during times of great crisis. It is how they responded to those difficulties that made them heroes in our eyes.

I hope that you will choose to be a hero in this time, because you will be needed. For decades, we have been exalting Christian celebrities and putting them up on pedestals. We watched them on television, we listened to their radio shows, we bought their books, and we attended their megachurches. We sent them lots and lots of our money, and we relied on them to do all the ministering.

That time has now come to an end. The era of the Christian celebrity is fading away, and now God is raising up an army. In this next move of God, ordinary people like you and like me are going to be the ones doing the ministering, and the only one that we are going to put up on a pedestal is Jesus Christ.

But if you are sitting around waiting for a pre-Tribulation rapture to pull you out of the action at any moment, you could potentially miss out on everything that God has planned for you.

So I hope that you will keep reading, because we are going to take a hard look at what the Bible really has to say about the timing of the rapture.

Hopefully by the time you are done reading what I have to share, your outlook on the future will be radically changed. Once you understand what God has planned, there is no way in the world that you should be looking to the future with fear.

What are you living for right now?

If you are living for material possessions and the pleasures of this world, the coming years are going to be extremely traumatic for you.

But if you are living for Jesus Christ, the years ahead are going to provide countless opportunities. It has been said that it doesn't matter how you start – what matters is how you finish. And maybe up until now you are disappointed in how your life has turned out and what you have done for God.

Perhaps you have been deeply scarred by things that have happened to you in the past. Perhaps you feel that you are so broken that you could never amount to anything. Well, the truth is that God can take the broken pieces of your life and turn them into a beautiful thing. He has done it for me, and He can do it for you. And even as the world falls apart all around you during the years that are ahead, God can turn you into the person that He always wanted you to be, and He can use you in ways that you never even imagined were possible.

There is nobody that is beyond hope, and there is not a single person on this planet that is out of the reach of my Jesus. And as we enter the darkest time this planet has ever seen, we are going to learn to love one another, and we are truly going to be the light of the world.

So please don't worry about what the future will bring. We serve the One that created all things, and the future is in His hands. The greatest time of victory the church has ever known is coming, and by the power of the Holy Spirit we will shake this world to the core.

God is in control, He has a plan, and nothing ever happens that takes Him by surprise. He knows every hair on your head and every breath that you take. And nothing is coming that you can't handle as long as you trust in Him.

With that being said, let's continue our examination of the timing of the rapture...

-CHAPTER THREE-

What Exactly Is "The Rapture"?

After writing a sizable portion of this book, it struck me that unless the reader has an extensive understanding of Bible prophecy already that it may be difficult to understand some of the things that I am explaining. So in this chapter I am going to define some of the most important terms that I am going to be using in this book, and I will be covering some of the basics of Bible prophecy. If you have already been studying what the Bible has to say about "the last days" for many years, you can probably skim this chapter and move on to chapter four. I just want everyone to be on the same page so that nobody will be totally lost once I start discussing more complex topics.

As I mentioned already, the term "the rapture" is never found in the Bible. But I do believe that the term is useful, and virtually all evangelical Christians understand that it is referring to the resurrection of the dead at the return of Christ.

In 1 Thessalonians 4, 1 Corinthians 15, Matthew 24, Mark 13, Revelation 14 and elsewhere, we are told about a day when Jesus will come back and gather believers to Himself. All of those Scriptures contain at least some of the following elements – Jesus descends from heaven and is seen in the clouds above our planet, there is the blowing of a great trumpet, dead believers are bodily resurrected and gathered to Him, living believers instantly have their physical bodies transformed without dying, and from that point forward we will be with the Lord forever.

Whenever you see the term "the rapture" in this book or elsewhere, I want you to remember that you could replace that term with "the resurrection". Just as Jesus rose from the dead, so will eventually all believers. The following comes out of 1 Corinthians 15...

20 But now is Christ risen from the dead, and become the firstfruits of them that slept.

21 For since by man came death, by man came also the resurrection of the dead.

22 For as in Adam all die, even so in Christ shall all be made alive.

23 But every man in his own order: Christ the firstfruits; **afterward they that are Christ's at his coming.**

Every believer should be looking forward to this day. It is the day when we will receive what we have been waiting for.

And the Bible actually contains far more prophecies about the second coming of Christ than it does about His first coming. All of human history is heading for a crescendo, and I believe that we are the generation that is going to get to see these things come to pass.

The Bible also speaks about a great time of trouble that will take place immediately before the return of Jesus. This period of time is commonly referred to as "the Tribulation" or "the Great Tribulation". Most Bible prophecy scholars teach that this is a seven year period that corresponds with Daniels 70th week (Daniel 9:24-27). It is also known in the Scriptures as "the Time of Jacob's Trouble".

There are others that teach that the Tribulation is only three and a half years long, but almost everyone agrees that the last three and a half years before Jesus returns at the Battle of Armageddon begin with the "abomination of desolation" that is mentioned in Matthew 24, Mark 13, Daniel 9 and Daniel 12.

Traditionally, there have been four main schools of thought regarding the timing of the rapture. Those that believe in a pre-Tribulation rapture believe that Jesus will come back and take believers to heaven prior to the beginning of the seven year Tribulation period. Those that are "left behind" will struggle to survive in a world gone mad, and there will be some that will turn to the Lord during this time period. After the seven years are over, Jesus comes back with the armies of heaven, defeats the Antichrist, and sets up His kingdom for a thousand years.

What I have just briefly outlined is what the vast majority of evangelical Christians in America today believe. It is taught in most evangelical Christian seminaries, it is all over Christian television and radio, and there are hundreds of prominent books that push this doctrine.

Personally, this is what I believed when I was growing up. Everyone else trusted what "the experts" were saying, and so I did too.

Another school of thought regarding the timing of the rapture is the mid-Tribulation view. This has become more popular in recent years, and I have seen quite a number of variations on it. Most of the variations are actually very similar to what pre-Trib scholars teach, except that the rapture is placed on or near the midpoint of the Tribulation.

The third school of thought, the "pre-wrath" viewpoint, has also gained in popularity in recent years. This school of thought rejects a pre-Tribulation rapture, and it emphasizes that the rapture must take place before the wrath of God is poured out on humanity. There are some "pre-wrathers" that also place the rapture at the midpoint of the Tribulation, but there are others that believe that it will happen somewhere during the last three and a half years. Usually those that hold to a pre-wrath view tend to believe that it will take place either at or near the end of the seal judgments.

The fourth school of thought is the post-Tribulation view. This has been the majority position throughout most of church history, and it lines up with all of the passages in the Bible that tell us that we will be gathered by the Lord once the Tribulation is over.

Of course there are multiple variations on this position as well, and some of them are very unusual. For instance, some "post-Tribbers" do not believe that there will be a rapture of believers at all. Instead, they believe that it is actually the unbelievers that are removed.

And of course there are other theories that I haven't even mentioned in this chapter. I get sent stuff all the time, and some of it is quite outlandish. People come up with all sorts of charts and graphs to explain their pet theories, but the more diagrams they come up with, the more confusing things seem to get.

Well, my goal in this book is to simplify things and make them very clear.

Hopefully by the time that I am done, you will see that the Bible does not make these things overly complicated.

I believe that God wants us to understand what is coming. That is why there is such a massive amount of material about "the last days" in the Word of God. He knows everything that is going to happen in advance, He is fully in control, and He wants us to have hope.

So I hope that you will continue to join me as we examine what the Bible really has to say about the timing of the rapture...

-CHAPTER FOUR-

The Parousia

There is so much confusion about the rapture in the Christian world today. Sadly, part of the problem has to do with our various Bible translations. Many of them are often vague or inaccurate, and they can leave people with the wrong impression.

When you examine the Scriptures in the original languages, things become much clearer. In this chapter, we are going to take a look at a Greek word that is more closely associated with the return of Jesus Christ than any other in the entire Bible. It is the Greek word "**parousia**", and according to Wikipedia it means "presence, arrival, or official visit". For example, when Pope Francis recently made his official visit to the United States, the ancient Greeks would have likely used the term "parousia" to describe what was happening.

Strong's Bible Dictionary says "parousia" can mean "presence", "the coming", "arrival" or "advent". In the King James version, this word is translated as "presence" twice, and the other 22 times that it is used it is translated as "coming". Overall, the word is used 24 times in the New Testament, and 16 of those instances have to do with the second coming of Jesus.

As I will explain below, the "parousia" and the rapture are very closely linked in the Scriptures. For example, if you ask most Christians where the rapture can be found in the Bible, the first place they will take you is 1 Thessalonians chapter 4. In this passage, we are told that the rapture takes place at the coming ("parousia") of the Lord. This is what 1 Thessalonians 4:14-17 says...

14 For if we believe that Jesus died and rose again, even so them also which sleep in Jesus will God bring with him.

*15 For this we say unto you by the word of the Lord, that we which are alive and remain unto the coming ("**parousia**") of the Lord shall not prevent them which are asleep.*

16 For the Lord himself shall descend from heaven with a shout, with the voice of the archangel, and with the trump of God: and the dead in Christ shall rise first:

17 Then we which are alive and remain shall be caught up together with them in the clouds, to meet the Lord in the air: and so shall we ever be with the Lord.

Is there any question that the "parousia" and the rapture happen at the same time in this passage?

Of course not.

So let's move on to another instance where the "parousia" and the rapture are linked. The next place most Christians will take you when you ask them where the rapture is described in the Bible is to 1 Corinthians chapter 15. That entire chapter focuses on the resurrection of believers from the dead (the rapture), and in 1 Corinthians 15:21-23 we are told that this happens at the "parousia"...

21 For since by man came death, by man came also the resurrection of the dead.

22 For as in Adam all die, even so in Christ shall all be made alive.

*23 But every man in his own order: Christ the firstfruits; afterward they that are Christ's at his coming ("**parousia**").*

Once again, when does the resurrection take place?

According to 1 Corinthians 15, it takes place at the coming ("parousia") of Christ.

Later on in that same chapter, we find the famous description of the resurrection (the rapture) that so many people love to quote. This is what 1 Corinthians 15:51-53 says...

51 Behold, I shew you a mystery; We shall not all sleep, but we shall all be changed,

52 In a moment, in the twinkling of an eye, at the last trump: for the trumpet shall sound, and the dead shall be raised incorruptible, and we shall be changed.

53 For this corruptible must put on incorruption, and this mortal must put on immortality.

Did you notice that 1 Thessalonians 4 and I Corinthians 15 both mentioned a trumpet?

This is something that we will be exploring a bit later on in this book. For now, I just want you to notice that little detail.

In Matthew 24, we also find the Greek word "parousia" being used. In fact, it is used **four times** in this chapter alone. In Matthew 24:3, the disciples of Jesus specifically ask Him when the "parousia" will happen...

*3 And as he sat upon the mount of Olives, the disciples came unto him privately, saying, Tell us, when shall these things be? and what shall be the sign of thy coming ("**parousia**"), and of the end of the world?*

And of course Jesus spends much of the rest of the chapter describing things that will happen just prior to His return.

Finally, in verse 27 Jesus gets to the "parousia", and in verse 29 we are told that it will take place "immediately after the tribulation of those days"...

*27 For as the lightning cometh out of the east, and shineth even unto the west; so shall also the coming ("**parousia**") of the Son of man be.*

28 For wheresoever the carcase is, there will the eagles be gathered together.

*29 **Immediately after the tribulation of those days** shall the sun be darkened, and the moon shall not give her light, and the stars shall fall from heaven, and the powers of the heavens shall be shaken:*

30 And then shall appear the sign of the Son of man in heaven: and then shall all the tribes of the earth mourn, and they shall see the Son of man coming in the clouds of heaven with power and great glory.

31 And he shall send his angels with a great sound of a trumpet, and they shall gather together his elect from the four winds, from one end of heaven to the other.

Obviously this does not fit into a pre-Trib paradigm, so they spend a tremendous amount of time and effort trying to explain how this coming which takes place "after the tribulation of those days" is different from the rapture.

But 1 Thessalonians 4, 1 Corinthians 15 and Matthew 24 all say that the rapture happens at the "parousia".

Is the Bible trying to trick us by using the exact same Greek word in all three instances?

No, of course the Bible is not trying to trick us. It is being exceedingly clear, but those that hold to the theory of a pre-Trib rapture do not want to hear what it is saying.

Later on in Matthew 24, the word "parousia" is used two more times. And as you can see below, once again Jesus tells us that the "parousia" and the rapture are connected. This is what Matthew 24:37-41 says...

*37 But as the days of Noah were, so shall also the coming ("**parousia**") of the Son of man be.*

38 For as in the days that were before the flood they were eating and drinking, marrying and giving in marriage, until the day that Noe entered into the ark,

*39 And knew not until the flood came, and took them all away; so shall also the coming ("**parousia**") of the Son of man be.*

40 Then shall two be in the field; the one shall be taken, and the other left.

41 Two women shall be grinding at the mill; the one shall be taken, and the other left.

So when are people "left behind"?

According to Jesus in Matthew 24, the rapture happens at His coming ("**parousia**"), and His coming ("**parousia**") occurs "immediately after the tribulation of those days".

Why do we refuse to believe the simple words of Jesus?

He wants us to know what to look for before He comes back so that we will not be deceived. But by twisting His words, those that advocate a pre-Trib rapture are leading millions astray.

The Apostle Paul specifically warned about this in 2 Thessalonians. In 2 Thessalonians 2:1-4, we are once again told that the rapture happens at the "parousia", and Paul lists certain events which must happen before the "parousia" takes place...

*Now we beseech you, brethren, by the coming ("**parousia**") of our Lord Jesus Christ, and by **our gathering together unto him**,*

2 That ye be not soon shaken in mind, or be troubled, neither by spirit, nor by word, nor by letter as from us, as that the day of Christ is at hand.

*3 **Let no man deceive you** by any means: **for that day shall not come, except there come a falling away first, and that man of sin be revealed**, the son of perdition;*

4 Who opposeth and exalteth himself above all that is called God, or that is worshipped; so that he as God sitteth in the temple of God, shewing himself that he is God.

Could the Bible be any clearer?

According to the Apostle Paul, there should not be any confusion regarding the timing of the rapture. Instead of coming before the Tribulation, it comes after a falling away takes place and the man of sin (the Antichrist) is revealed. Paul explains that we will know exactly who the Antichrist is because he is going to actually go into a rebuilt Jewish temple and proclaim himself to be God.

And Matthew 24 tells us that this event ("the abomination of desolation") begins a period of great tribulation unlike anything the world has ever seen before. At the end of that period of great tribulation, the rapture will take place at the coming ("**parousia**") of the Lord. (Matthew 24:29-31)

Going back to 2 Thessalonians 2, the Apostle Paul tells us something else very important about the "parousia". And in this case, it totally destroys all theories that place the rapture before the end of the Tribulation period. In verses 5 through 8, the Apostle Paul continues his discussion about the Antichrist, and we are told that the final confrontation between Jesus and the Antichrist comes at the "parousia"...

5 Remember ye not, that, when I was yet with you, I told you these things?

6 And now ye know what withholdeth that he might be revealed in his time.

7 For the mystery of iniquity doth already work: only he who now letteth will let, until he be taken out of the way.

*8 And then shall that Wicked be revealed, whom the Lord shall consume with the spirit of his mouth, and shall destroy with the brightness of his coming ("**parousia**")*

Of course we know from Revelation 19 and elsewhere that the final confrontation between the Lord Jesus and the Antichrist comes at the very end of the Tribulation period.

So why is there so much confusion over all this? And as you will see in later chapters, this is just a small piece of the puzzle. The truth is that there is an overwhelming amount of evidence that points to the fact that the rapture comes immediately after the Tribulation.

I truly hope that I have explained these things clearly enough so that you can understand. In all of the passages that we have looked at, we are told that the rapture happens at the "parousia", and Matthew 24 and 2 Thessalonians 2 are exceedingly clear in telling us that the "parousia" takes place at the end of the Tribulation.

In the next chapter, I would like to take a look at another very important clue that clearly indicates that the rapture comes at the conclusion of the Tribulation period...

-CHAPTER FIVE-

The Day Of The Lord Cometh

22 times in the Old Testament, the phrase "the Day of the Lord" is used. The Apostle Paul was trained at the feet of a famous Jewish rabbi named Gamaliel, and from a very early age he was immersed in the Old Testament Scriptures. So when he decided to use the phrase "the Day of the Lord" in 1 Thessalonians 5, he knew **exactly** what he was doing.

Below, you will find the end of 1 Thessalonians 4 and the beginning of 1 Thessalonians 5. In ancient times, there were no chapter divisions in the New Testament. Most people don't realize that they were added much later for clarity. As modern believers, we often stop reading when we come to the end of a chapter, but often an important discussion is carried over into subsequent chapters. One of these instances is at the end of 1 Thessalonians 4...

15 For this we say unto you by the word of the Lord, that we which are alive and remain unto the coming of the Lord shall not prevent them which are asleep.

16 For the Lord himself shall descend from heaven with a shout, with the voice of the archangel, and with the trump of God: and the dead in Christ shall rise first:

17 Then we which are alive and remain shall be caught up together with them in the clouds, to meet the Lord in the air: and so shall we ever be with the Lord.

18 Wherefore comfort one another with these words.

1 But of the times and the seasons, brethren, ye have no need that I write unto you.

*2 For yourselves know perfectly **that the day of the Lord so cometh as a thief in the night**.*

3 For when they shall say, Peace and safety; then sudden destruction cometh upon them, as travail upon a woman with child; and they shall not escape.

4 But ye, brethren, are not in darkness, that that day should overtake you as a thief.

5 Ye are all the children of light, and the children of the day: we are not of the night, nor of darkness.

In a future chapter, I will discuss the phrase "a thief in the night" extensively. For now, I just want you to notice what comes "as a thief in the night".

As I was growing up, I was taught that the rapture comes as a thief in the night, and that is true. The Apostle Paul is clearly talking about the rapture in this passage. But in verse 2 of chapter 5 he tells us that this rapture that he has just described will come at a time known as "the Day of the Lord".

In 2 Peter 3, the Apostle Peter also tells us that the Day of the Lord will come as "a thief in the night"...

*10 But **the day of the Lord will come as a thief in the night**; in the which the heavens shall pass away with a great noise, and the elements shall melt with fervent heat, the earth also and the works that are therein shall be burned up.*

11 Seeing then that all these things shall be dissolved, what manner of persons ought ye to be in all holy conversation and godliness,

12 Looking for and hasting unto the coming of the day of God, wherein the heavens being on fire shall be dissolved, and the elements shall melt with fervent heat?

But that doesn't sound like a pre-Tribulation rapture to me. None of the rapture movies that I ever saw had scenes where the heavens passed away with a great noise or the elements melted with fervent heat.

Could it be possible that the way that we have been imagining the rapture is totally wrong?

Let's take a look at a couple of passages from the Old Testament that clearly describe the coming of "the Day of the Lord". I would like to begin with the first four verses of Zechariah 14...

*Behold, **the day of the Lord cometh**, and thy spoil shall be divided in the midst of thee.*

2 For I will gather all nations against Jerusalem to battle; and the city shall be taken, and the houses rifled, and the women ravished; and half of the city shall go forth into captivity, and the residue of the people shall not be cut off from the city.

3 Then shall the Lord go forth, and fight against those nations, as when he fought in the day of battle.

*4 **And his feet shall stand in that day upon the mount of Olives**, which is before Jerusalem on the east, and the mount of Olives shall cleave in the midst thereof toward the east and toward the west, and there shall be a very great valley; and half of the mountain shall remove toward the north, and half of it toward the south.*

When the Day of the Lord comes, Zechariah says that the Lord's feet will stand upon the Mount of Olives. And this makes perfect sense, because in Acts 1 we are told that Jesus ascended from the Mount of Olives and will return in like manner...

9 And when he had spoken these things, while they beheld, he was taken up; and a cloud received him out of their sight.

10 And while they looked stedfastly toward heaven as he went up, behold, two men stood by them in white apparel;

*11 **Which also said, Ye men of Galilee, why stand ye gazing up into heaven? this same Jesus, which is taken up from you into heaven, shall so come in like manner as ye have seen him go into heaven.***

12 Then returned they unto Jerusalem from the mount called Olivet, which is from Jerusalem a sabbath day's journey.

Everyone agrees that Jesus does not physically touch down on this planet on the Mount of Olives until the end of the Tribulation period. And Zechariah 14 tells us that this happens at the coming of the Day of the Lord.

But if the rapture also happens at the coming of the Day of the Lord, that puts it at the end of the Tribulation.

Hmm – very, very interesting.

Now let's take a look at the first eleven verses of Joel 2 where the Day of the Lord is once again described in quite a bit of detail...

Blow ye the trumpet in Zion, and sound an alarm in my holy mountain: let all the inhabitants of the land tremble:

for the day of the Lord cometh, for it is nigh at hand;

2 A day of darkness and of gloominess, a day of clouds and of thick darkness, as the morning spread upon the mountains: a great people and a strong; there hath not been ever the like, neither shall be any more after it, even to the years of many generations.

3 A fire devoureth before them; and behind them a flame burneth: the land is as the garden of Eden before them, and behind them a desolate wilderness; yea, and nothing shall escape them.

4 The appearance of them is as the appearance of horses; and as horsemen, so shall they run.

5 Like the noise of chariots on the tops of mountains shall they leap, like the noise of a flame of fire that devoureth the stubble, as a strong people set in battle array.

6 Before their face the people shall be much pained: all faces shall gather blackness.

7 They shall run like mighty men; they shall climb the wall like men of war; and they shall march every one on his ways, and they shall not break their ranks:

8 Neither shall one thrust another; they shall walk every one in his path: and when they fall upon the sword, they shall not be wounded.

9 They shall run to and fro in the city; they shall run upon the wall, they shall climb up upon the houses; they shall enter in at the windows like a thief.

10 The earth shall quake before them; the heavens shall tremble: **the sun and the moon shall be dark, and the stars shall withdraw their shining***:*

11 **And the Lord shall utter his voice before his army***: for his camp is very great: for he is strong that executeth his word:* **for the day of the Lord is great and very terrible***; and who can abide it?*

This passage should be setting off all sorts of alarm bells for you. In these verses, we see the Lord Jesus personally leading the greatest army of all time on horses back to Zion (Jerusalem).

So when does the Lord personally lead an indestructible conquering army on horses back to Jerusalem?

This comes at the end of the Tribulation period of course. What you just read out of Joel 2 should immediately remind you of Revelation 19...

11 And I saw heaven opened, and behold a white horse; and he that sat upon him was called Faithful and True, and in righteousness he doth judge and make war.

12 His eyes were as a flame of fire, and on his head were many crowns; and he had a name written, that no man knew, but he himself.

13 And he was clothed with a vesture dipped in blood: and his name is called The Word of God.

14 **And the armies which were in heaven followed him upon white horses, clothed in fine linen, white and clean***.*

15 And out of his mouth goeth a sharp sword, that with it he should smite the nations: and he shall rule them with a rod of iron: and he treadeth the winepress of the fierceness and wrath of Almighty God.

16 And he hath on his vesture and on his thigh a name written, King Of Kings, And Lord Of Lords.

Joel 2 and Revelation 19 are both accounts of the physical return of Jesus Christ with His army to this planet at the end of the Tribulation period.

And it is important to note that Jesus specifically linked Joel chapter 2 to the timing of the rapture in Matthew chapter 24. In fact, in many Bibles there is a little footnote after Matthew 24:29 alerting the reader to the fact that Jesus appears to be quoting Joel 2:10. And as we have already seen, Matthew 24 tells us that the rapture comes "immediately after the tribulation of those days"...

*29 Immediately after the tribulation of those days shall **the sun be darkened, and the moon shall not give her light, and the stars shall fall from heaven**, and the powers of the heavens shall be shaken:*

30 And then shall appear the sign of the Son of man in heaven: and then shall all the tribes of the earth mourn, and they shall see the Son of man coming in the clouds of heaven with power and great glory.

31 And he shall send his angels with a great sound of a trumpet, and they shall gather together his elect from the four winds, from one end of heaven to the other.

Go back and look at Joel 2:10 again. There is a reason why Jesus is pointing us to this verse. He wanted us to know that the rapture will occur during the coming of the Day of the Lord described in Joel chapter 2.

And we find another very similar Old Testament passage in Isaiah 13...

9 **Behold, the day of the Lord cometh**, *cruel both with wrath and fierce anger, to lay the land desolate: and he shall destroy the sinners thereof out of it.*

10 **For the stars of heaven and the constellations thereof shall not give their light: the sun shall be darkened in his going forth, and the moon shall not cause her light to shine.**

11 *And I will punish the world for their evil, and the wicked for their iniquity; and I will cause the arrogancy of the proud to cease, and will lay low the haughtiness of the terrible.*

12 *I will make a man more precious than fine gold; even a man than the golden wedge of Ophir.*

13 *Therefore I will shake the heavens, and the earth shall remove out of her place, in the wrath of the Lord of hosts, and in the day of his fierce anger.*

Just like in Joel, we are told that when the Day of the Lord comes the sun will be darkened, the moon will not give her light, and the activity of the stars will be disrupted.

And all of this lines up perfectly with what the Apostle Paul was trying to tell us in 1 Thessalonians. When the Apostle Paul used the phrase "the Day of the Lord" in 1 Thessalonians 5, he was very well aware of what Zechariah, Joel and other Old Testament prophets had written about it.

So it should be exceedingly clear what Paul was telling us about the timing of the rapture.

Instead of coming before the Tribulation as so many teach, the Apostle Paul told us that it happens at the coming of "the Day of the Lord" which comes immediately after the Tribulation period. This also happens to be perfectly consistent with what Jesus taught. In Matthew 24, Jesus pointed to the passage about "the Day of the Lord" in Joel chapter 2, and just like the Apostle Paul He identified the coming of "the Day of the Lord" as the time when the rapture happens.

In the next chapter, I would like to explore what Jesus had to say in Matthew 24 quite a bit more...

-CHAPTER SIX-

After The Tribulation Of Those Days...

God is not trying to confuse us. Yes, there are very deep and complex things in the Word of God, but the most important truths in the Scriptures are very clear. God intended for people living at different times and in different places all throughout history to be able to understand them. For instance, the fact that Jesus died on the cross for our sins is abundantly clear when one reads through the New Testament. When it comes to the things that we really need to know, God is not playing hide and seek with us.

This is definitely true when it comes to the second coming of our Messiah. Many Bible prophecy teachers today require incredibly complicated charts and graphs to even answer the most basic questions about the things to come. But the basic truths about the last days are not that complex.

In Matthew chapter 24, the disciples of Jesus came to Him and asked about the signs that we should expect to see just before His return...

And as he sat upon the mount of Olives, the disciples came unto him privately, saying, Tell us, when shall these things be? and what shall be the sign of thy coming, and of the end of the world?

Similar accounts can be found in Mark chapter 13 and Luke chapter 21. In all three instances, Jesus discusses a chain of dramatic events that will happen just before He comes back, and He tells us that His return will occur immediately after a period of great tribulation has finished.

In this chapter, I am going to focus on Matthew 24, but many of the exact same things that I will be saying about Matthew

24 could also be said about Mark 13 and Luke 21. Jesus didn't want us to be fooled when it came to His second coming. In fact, in verse 4 of Matthew 24 Jesus specifically says "take heed that no man deceive you". He told us what was going to happen ahead of time so that we would not be afraid and so that we would not be led astray.

So exactly what should we be looking for? In verses 5 through 14, Jesus describes what things will generally be like just prior to His return...

5 For many shall come in my name, saying, I am Christ; and shall deceive many.

6 And ye shall hear of wars and rumours of wars: see that ye be not troubled: for all these things must come to pass, but the end is not yet.

7 For nation shall rise against nation, and kingdom against kingdom: and there shall be famines, and pestilences, and earthquakes, in divers places.

8 All these are the beginning of sorrows.

9 Then shall they deliver you up to be afflicted, and shall kill you: and ye shall be hated of all nations for my name's sake.

10 And then shall many be offended, and shall betray one another, and shall hate one another.

11 And many false prophets shall rise, and shall deceive many.

12 And because iniquity shall abound, the love of many shall wax cold.

13 But he that shall endure unto the end, the same shall be saved.

14 And this gospel of the kingdom shall be preached in all the world for a witness unto all nations; and then shall the end come.

A number of these signs that Jesus discusses here could easily apply to just about any time throughout history. For example, there have always been false Christs running around, and I can't think of a time when our world has not seen "wars and rumors of wars". But the key is to look for all of them happening at the same time, and we should also expect these signs to increase in frequency and intensity.

Without a doubt, seismic activity on this planet is rising. During the 20th century, there were a total of 3,542 volcanic eruptions globally. That works out to approximately 35 eruptions per year. That may sound like a lot, but as I write this there are 37 volcanoes erupting around the world right now. In other words, the number of volcanoes erupting at this moment is greater than the 20th century's yearly average.

And all of the other signs that Jesus mentioned are present in our world today as well, but I expect that these "birth pains" will soon get a lot worse. I believe that the great war in the Middle East that many refer to as "the Psalm 83 war" is not too far in the future. I also believe that we are going to see global economic collapse, tremendous outbreaks of disease, and natural disasters of a magnitude that we have not seen since the days of Noah. So as bad as things are right now, the truth is that this is just the warm up act.

After the "beginning of sorrows" described in verses five through eight, Jesus tells us about a great persecution of believers that will take place. He explains that we "shall be hated of all nations for my name's sake" and that many of us will be killed. On a small scale this is already happening around the world, but what Jesus is speaking of here is much worse and it is global in scope.

Lastly, Jesus tells us that "this gospel of the kingdom shall be preached in all the world for a witness unto all nations; and then shall the end come." Never before in human history have we come so close to fulfilling the Great Commission, but we still have a lot of work to do. The good news is that ultimately it will happen. The gospel will be proclaimed in all the world, and I personally believe that a great harvest of souls is coming. I will have much more to say about this later in the book.

For now, I want you to focus on the pivot point that comes in verse 15. Jesus transitions from speaking in generalizations to speaking about a very specific event...

15 When ye therefore shall see the abomination of desolation, spoken of by Daniel the prophet, stand in the holy place, (whoso readeth, let him understand:)

Those listening to Jesus at that time would have immediately recognized what He was talking about. The abomination of desolation is first mentioned in the book of Daniel in chapter 9, and it falls right in the middle of "Daniel's 70th week". This is what Daniel 9:27 says...

27 And he shall confirm the covenant with many for one week: and in the midst of the week he shall cause the sacrifice and the oblation to cease, and for the overspreading of abominations he shall make it desolate, even until the consummation, and that determined shall be poured upon the desolate.

We also see the abomination of desolation mentioned in Daniel chapter 12...

11 And from the time that the daily sacrifice shall be taken away, and the abomination that maketh desolate set up, there shall be a thousand two hundred and ninety days.

Nearly all serious Bible prophecy experts agree that this event takes place at the middle of the seven year Tribulation period. If there was going to be a mid-Tribulation rapture, we would expect Jesus to instruct us to get ready to be gathered home once we see the abomination of desolation because He is about to come get us.

But that is not what we see at all. Instead, Jesus instructs believers that are living in Israel to flee to the mountains...

16 Then let them which be in Judaea flee into the mountains:

17 Let him which is on the housetop not come down to take any thing out of his house:

18 Neither let him which is in the field return back to take his clothes.

19 And woe unto them that are with child, and to them that give suck in those days!

20 But pray ye that your flight be not in the winter, neither on the sabbath day:

21 For then shall be great tribulation, such as was not since the beginning of the world to this time, no, nor ever shall be.

Now why in the world would He give us these instructions if the rapture was about to take place?

It simply would not make any sense.

And notice that in verse 20 Jesus is instructing those that are fleeing to "pray".

So who is He speaking to there – believers or non-believers?

He is speaking to believers of course.

Instead of being pulled out of here in a mid-Tribulation rapture, believers in the land of Israel are fleeing to the mountains because a period of "great tribulation" has begun. You can read more about this place of safety that believers are fleeing to at the end of Revelation 12...

13 And when the dragon saw that he was cast unto the earth, he persecuted the woman which brought forth the man child.

14 And to the woman were given two wings of a great eagle, that she might fly into the wilderness, into her place, where she is nourished for a time, and times, and half a time, from the face of the serpent.

15 And the serpent cast out of his mouth water as a flood after the woman, that he might cause her to be carried away of the flood.

16 And the earth helped the woman, and the earth opened her mouth, and swallowed up the flood which the dragon cast out of his mouth.

17 And the dragon was wroth with the woman, and went to make war with the remnant of her seed, which keep the commandments of God, and have the testimony of Jesus Christ.

After Satan realizes that he can't get at the believers that have fled to a place of safety in the wilderness, he goes after "the remnant of her seed, which keep the commandments of God, and have the testimony of Jesus Christ."

Now let me ask you another question – are those that "have the testimony of Jesus Christ" believers or non-believers?

Once again, the answer is quite obvious.

If there had been a mid-Tribulation rapture, those Christians would already be gone, but instead we find that they are still running around down on this planet.

If we just use a little common sense, the Bible is exceedingly clear.

Once we see the abomination of desolation, Jesus says that from that moment until His return will be the worst period of "tribulation" the world has ever seen or will ever see again. Essentially, it will be three and a half years of pure hell. Revelation 13 describes it as a time when the Antichrist will "make war with the saints", and that chapter also tells us that it will last for 42 months. This period of time will be far worse than the Great Depression, it will be far worse than the Holocaust, and it will be far worse than any war the world has ever experienced. I honestly believe that none of us really understands right now just how horrific it is going to be. In verse 22, Jesus tells us that unless the days were shortened "there should no flesh be saved".

The term "great tribulation" in verse 21 is made up of two Greek words. The first word is "megas" which means great, and the second word is "thlipsis" which is translated as "tribulation". This exact same Greek word, "thlipsis", is used just eight verses later in an absolutely critical passage...

*29 Immediately after the **tribulation** ("thlipsis") of those days shall the sun be darkened, and the moon shall not give her light, and the stars shall fall from heaven, and the powers of the heavens shall be shaken:*

30 And then shall appear the sign of the Son of man in heaven: and then shall all the tribes of the earth mourn, and they shall see the Son of man coming in the clouds of heaven with power and great glory.

31 And he shall send his angels with a great sound of a trumpet, and they shall gather together his elect from the four winds, from one end of heaven to the other.

In verse 29, "thlipsis" is once again translated in the King James Version as "tribulation". So there is no question what "tribulation" is being discussed here. It is the period of "great tribulation" that was just mentioned in verse 21. So this completely rules out a mid-Tribulation rapture.

The rapture does not come before "the tribulation of those days".

It comes immediately after.

I honestly do not understand why Bible scholars cannot seem to understand what "after the tribulation" means. Yes, I know that it does not fit with what they want to believe. But it is so abundantly clear, and it doesn't leave any margin for wiggle room.

So precisely what will happen "after the tribulation of those days"? Let's take another look at verses 30 and 31 of Matthew 24...

30 And then shall appear the sign of the Son of man in heaven: and then shall all the tribes of the earth mourn, and they shall see the Son of man coming in the clouds of heaven with power and great glory.

31 And he shall send his angels with a great sound of a trumpet, and they shall gather together his elect from the four winds, from one end of heaven to the other.

This is the event known as the rapture. Jesus comes in the clouds, a trumpet is blown, and believers are gathered to Him from all over the world. As we shall see in the next chapter, we find these exact same details in 1 Thessalonians chapter 4.

But before we move outside the gospels, let's take a look at what Mark and Luke have to say. This is the description of the rapture that we find in Mark 13...

24 But in those days, after that tribulation, the sun shall be darkened, and the moon shall not give her light,

25 And the stars of heaven shall fall, and the powers that are in heaven shall be shaken.

26 And then shall they see the Son of man coming in the clouds with great power and glory.

27 And then shall he send his angels, and shall gather together his elect from the four winds, from the uttermost part of the earth to the uttermost part of heaven.

There is no trumpet mentioned, but otherwise it is almost a carbon copy of what we just read in Matthew 24. And I find it particularly interesting that in verse 27 it tells us that the elect are gathered "from the uttermost part of the earth to the uttermost part of heaven". That means that all of us are gathered – the living and the dead.

And this is how the same event is described in Luke 21...

25 And there shall be signs in the sun, and in the moon, and in the stars; and upon the earth distress of nations, with perplexity; the sea and the waves roaring;

26 Men's hearts failing them for fear, and for looking after those things which are coming on the earth: for the powers of heaven shall be shaken.

27 And then shall they see the Son of man coming in a cloud with power and great glory.

Those that believe in a pre-Tribulation rapture somehow have to figure out a way for there to be a separate event seven years earlier in which Jesus also comes on the clouds, a trumpet is blown and believers (both living and dead) are gathered to Him.

When you talk to those that believe in a pre-Tribulation rapture, they can never take you to a verse that says that it will happen before the Tribulation because such a verse **does not exist**. Instead, they will give you all kinds of excuses, and they will pull out all sorts of charts and graphs, and they will start quoting all sorts of "experts", but they can never seem to give you a straight answer.

Well, in this book we are going to sort these things out. If there was going to be a pre-Tribulation rapture, Jesus would have told us about it. It would have been at the beginning of Matthew 24, Mark 13 and Luke 21 instead of at the end of each of those chapters.

Jesus was very clear that the rapture happens "after the tribulation of those days", and as we will see in the next chapter, this lines up perfectly with what the rest of the Bible says...

-CHAPTER SEVEN-

The Last Trumpet

Why is the blowing of a trumpet so prominently mentioned in 1 Thessalonians 4, 1 Corinthians 15 and Matthew 24? Could God be trying to tell us something?

In this chapter, you will see that all three passages are describing the future resurrection of believers at the rapture. And in all three passages God has left clues in His Word so that we would know that they are all describing the exact same event.

Here are the relevant verses from 1 Thessalonians 4 – I believe that many of you will already be extremely familiar with them...

14 For if we believe that Jesus died and rose again, even so them also which sleep in Jesus will God bring with him.

15 For this we say unto you by the word of the Lord, that we which are alive and remain unto the coming of the Lord shall not prevent them which are asleep.

*16 For the Lord himself shall descend from **heaven** with a shout, with the voice of the archangel, and **with the trump of God**: and the dead in Christ shall rise first:*

*17 Then we which are alive and remain shall be caught up together with them **in the clouds**, to meet the Lord in the air: and so shall we ever be with the Lord.*

18 Wherefore comfort one another with these words.

Now compare those verses to what we looked at earlier out of Matthew 24...

29 Immediately after the tribulation of those days shall the sun be darkened, and the moon shall not give her light, and the stars shall fall from heaven, and the powers of the heavens shall be shaken:

30 And then shall appear the sign of the Son of man in **heaven***: and then shall all the tribes of the earth mourn, and they shall see the Son of man coming* **in the clouds** *of* **heaven** *with power and great glory.*

31 And he shall send his angels **with a great sound of a trumpet***, and they shall gather together his elect from the four winds, from one end of* **heaven** *to the other.*

To even the most uninformed reader, the similarities are glaringly obvious. Jesus comes in the clouds, there is the sounding of a great trumpet, and believers from all over the world are gathered together to Him.

But in the Greek, the parallels are even more striking. For example, the word translated as "the clouds" in 1 Thessalonians 4:17 is the Greek word "nephele". In Matthew 24:30, we also see the Greek word "nephele" translated as "the clouds" in the King James version.

So the exact same word is used to describe where the events of both Matthew 24 and 1 Thessalonians 4 will take place.

Let's take a look at another example. In 1 Thessalonians 4:16, the Greek word "salpigx" is translated as "the trump" in the King James version. In Matthew 24, the Greek word "salpigx" is translated as "a trumpet".

So in both accounts we have the blowing of a great trumpet, and the exact same Greek word is used in both instances.

Here is one more example of this phenomenon. In 1 Thessalonians 4:16 the Greek word "ouranos" is translated as "heaven" in the King James version, and in both Matthew 24:30 and Matthew 24:31 the Greek word "ouranos" is also translated in the King James version as "heaven".

Why do these passages have so many Greek words in common?

It is because they are both describing the exact same event, which comes at the end of the Tribulation period.

In both instances, the Lord Jesus descends from heaven, angels are involved in the proceedings, a trumpet is sounded and believers are gathered from all over the planet to meet the Lord.

In 1 Corinthians chapter 15, we find another passage that describes this exact same event...

50 Now this I say, brethren, that flesh and blood cannot inherit the kingdom of God; neither doth corruption inherit incorruption.

51 Behold, I shew you a mystery; We shall not all sleep, but we shall all be changed,

*52 In a moment, in the twinkling of an eye, **at the last trump**: for the trumpet shall sound, and the dead shall be raised incorruptible, and we shall be changed.*

53 For this corruptible must put on incorruption, and this mortal must put on immortality.

54 So when this corruptible shall have put on incorruption, and this mortal shall have put on immortality, then shall be brought to pass the saying that is written, Death is swallowed up in victory.

In verse 52, we once again find the Greek word "salpigx", and in this case it is translated as "trump". In fact, the entire Greek phrase used there is "en eschatos salpigx" which is rendered as "at the last trump" in the King James version.

So just like in I Thessalonians 4 and Matthew 24, the resurrection of believers, both living and dead, is portrayed as happening in conjunction with the blowing of a great trumpet. But in this instance we get the additional detail of it being "at the **last** trump".

This presents quite a problem for those that believe in a pre-Tribulation or a mid-Tribulation rapture, because lots of trumpets are blown in the book of Revelation.

If indeed the rapture is "at the last trump" as the Word of God clearly states, that would seem to imply a series of trumpet blasts. You see, you can't have a "last trump" without a "first trump", etc.

So how do pre-Trib and mid-Trib scholars attempt to get around this?

Well, I have seen all kinds of wild theories, and most of them are completely ridiculous.

The best of the theories is the one that tries to link "the last trump" with the last trumpet blast on the Feast of Trumpets (Rosh Hashanah).

On Rosh Hashanah, traditionally there is a series of 100 shofar blasts. The very last of these trumpet blasts is known as the "Tekiah Gedolah" or "the last trumpet". So the idea is that this "last trumpet" is the "last trumpet" referred to in 1 Corinthians chapter 15, and that may indeed be the case.

But I believe that there is more to it than that. Yes, I do believe that the rapture will fall on the Feast of Trumpets in some future year. In a chapter later in this book I am going to go over this in quite a bit of detail. The Biblical festivals that fall in the spring were fulfilled to the day by the first coming of Jesus, and I believe that the Biblical festivals that happen in the fall will also be fulfilled to the day by the second coming of Jesus.

However, I am fully convinced that this "last trumpet" also refers to the series of trumpets that we find in the book of Revelation, and this is something that I will expound upon in the next chapter...

-CHAPTER EIGHT-

The Rapture Is In The Book Of Revelation

For most of my life, I believed in a pre-Tribulation rapture. I read books published by the most famous pre-Trib experts in the world, I watched their television shows, and I purchased their conference DVDs. There were always passages in the Bible that troubled me, but when I was younger I assumed that the experts knew much more than I did and that I should trust them.

That was a big mistake.

In this day and age, it is absolutely imperative that we all learn to think for ourselves. So many Christians today let the "experts" do their thinking for them. And I certainly hope that you don't take the things that I have to share on blind faith. Be a good Berean and dig into the Scriptures for yourself to see if these things are true.

When we stand before the Lord, we aren't going to be able to blame someone else for the things that we personally believed and taught. So make absolutely certain that what you believe lines up with the Word of God.

When I was younger, I could never understand why the rapture was not clearly described in the book of Revelation. It is certainly going to be one of the most dramatic moments in human history, and it is the moment that believers have been eagerly anticipating for centuries. So it always seemed quite odd to me that it had been completely left out of the one book in the Bible that is all about the end times.

Of course today many pre-Trib and mid-Trib "experts" are suggesting that the rapture is implied in Revelation 4 and/or Revelation 7, and I will deal with those instances in later chapters. But even they will admit that the rapture is not clearly described in detail in the book of Revelation, and this puzzles many of them.

Well, the reason why none of those experts can seem to find the rapture clearly described in the book of Revelation is because they have been looking in the wrong place.

As I studied these things years ago, I began wondering if the trumpet blasts mentioned in Matthew 24, 1 Thessalonians 4 and I Corinthians 15 had anything to do with the seven trumpets of the book of Revelation.

Since 1 Corinthians 15 says that the rapture comes at "the last trump", one would expect to find the rapture described in the book of Revelation at the same time the last trumpet is sounded in Revelation chapter 11 or shortly thereafter, but before the first vial judgment is poured out in Revelation chapter 16.

And guess what?

That is precisely what we see.

First, let's take a look at what is said immediately following the sounding of the seventh trumpet in Revelation 11...

15 And the seventh angel sounded; and there were great voices in heaven, saying, The kingdoms of this world are become the kingdoms of our Lord, and of his Christ; and he shall reign for ever and ever.

16 And the four and twenty elders, which sat before God on their seats, fell upon their faces, and worshipped God,

17 Saying, We give thee thanks, O Lord God Almighty, which art, and wast, and art to come; because thou hast taken to thee thy great power, and hast reigned.

18 And the nations were angry, and thy wrath is come, **and the time of the dead, that they should be judged, and that thou shouldest give reward unto thy servants the prophets, and to the saints, and them that fear thy name, small and great;** *and shouldest destroy them which destroy the earth.*

The phrase that I want to focus on for just a moment is "the time of the dead".

I must have gone over that verse hundreds of times before, but that phrase never really registered with me, and I have never heard a single Bible prophecy expert or pastor teach on it.

So what exactly is "the time of the dead"?

Is it the time for the dead to stay dead?

Is it the time for the dead to roll over in their graves?

No, of course the only logical answer is that it is the time for the dead to come back to life!

The truth is that you only have to think about it for a couple of seconds before you come to the inescapable conclusion that this is talking about the resurrection. And the phrases that immediately follow confirm this...

...that they should be judged, and that thou shouldest give reward unto thy servants the prophets, and to the saints, and them that fear thy

name, small and great; *and shouldest destroy them which destroy the earth.*

When does the Lord Jesus reward His servants?

It is when He returns of course. Just check out Matthew 16:27…

For the Son of man shall come in the glory of his Father with his angels; and then he shall **reward** *every man according to his works.*

And in Revelation 22:12, the Lord Jesus tells us this…

12 And, behold, I come quickly; and my **reward** *is with me, to give every man according as his work shall be.*

We are rewarded at His coming, and when the seventh trumpet is sounded in Revelation 11 we are told that the time for that has come!

There are a couple of other things that I want you to notice in Revelation 11. This time let's look at how verses 15 through 18 are rendered in the MEV…

15 The seventh angel sounded, and there were loud voices in heaven, saying:

"The kingdoms of the world have become the kingdoms of our Lord, and of His Christ, and He shall reign forever and ever."

16 And the twenty-four elders, who sat before God on their thrones, fell on their faces and worshipped God,

17 saying: "We give You thanks, O Lord God Almighty, who is and was and who is to come, because You have taken Your great power and **begun to reign.**

*18 The nations were angry, and **Your wrath has come**, and the time has come for the dead to be judged, and to reward Your servants the prophets and the saints and those who fear Your name, small and great, and to destroy those who destroy the earth."*

When the seventh angel blows his trumpet, he declares that the "kingdoms of the world have become the kingdoms of our Lord, and of His Christ".

And in verse 17, the 24 elders declare that God has now "begun to reign".

Personally, I believe that what we see here is a declaration that the seven year Tribulation period has ended and that the 1000 year reign of Christ has begun. The very first thing that Jesus does when He begins to reign is to gather His bride to Himself, and after that the wrath of God is poured out in preparation for the triumphant return of Christ to this planet. We see a reference to the pouring out of this wrath in verse 18. I believe that this is a direct reference to the upcoming vial judgments.

Following this incredible series of declarations in Revelation chapter 11, we find an actual physical description of the rapture in Revelation chapter 14. And this makes perfect sense because Revelation 14 comes immediately after the last trumpet has been blown, but before the first vial judgment is poured out in Revelation 16.

In Revelation chapter 14 we read the following...

*14 And I looked, and behold a **white cloud**, and upon the cloud **one sat like unto the Son of man**, having on his head **a golden crown**, and in his hand a sharp sickle.*

*15 And another angel came out of the temple, crying with a loud voice to him that sat on the cloud, Thrust in thy sickle, and reap: for the time is come for thee to reap; **for the harvest of the earth is ripe**.*

*16 And he that **sat on the cloud** thrust in his sickle on the earth; and **the earth was reaped**.*

In verse 14, the word "cloud" and the phrase "the cloud" are both translations of the Greek word "nephele". In the previous chapter, we discussed how this Greek word was also used in both Matthew 24 and 1 Thessalonians 4.

Who is it that comes in the clouds?

I am only going to give you one guess, and if you guessed anyone other than Jesus you guessed wrong.

And the individual doing the harvesting here is referred to as "the Son of Man". In the Greek, the phrase "huios anthropos" is used. That is the exact same Greek phrase that Jesus used twice to refer to Himself in Matthew 24...

*30 And then shall appear the sign of **the Son of man** in heaven: and then shall all the tribes of the earth mourn, and they shall see **the Son of man** coming in the clouds of heaven with power and great glory.*

In addition, we see that the individual doing the harvesting in Revelation 14 is wearing a crown.

Angels don't wear crowns.

Only the King wears a crown.

Is there anyone out there that has any doubt that this passage is referring to Jesus?

If there is, please email me, because I would love to hear your reasoning.

In Revelation chapter 14, the one described as "the Son of Man" is conducting a harvest.

So precisely what would Jesus be harvesting?

In the King James version, the word "harvest" is only used eight times in the New Testament. In each instance, it refers to a harvest of souls. For example, just check out what it says in John 4:35...

35 Say not ye, There are yet four months, and then cometh harvest? behold, I say unto you, Lift up your eyes, and look on the fields; for they are white already to harvest.

If Jesus has not come back to gather believers, what else has He come to harvest in Revelation 14?

Is He harvesting corn?

Is He harvesting wheat?

The answer, of course, is completely obvious to anyone that doesn't have a theological axe to grind.

The rapture is right there in the book of Revelation exactly where we would expect it to be.

After this rapture in Revelation chapter 14, there is no mention of any more believers on this planet until we triumphantly return with Jesus in Revelation chapter 19.

Instead, what we do find is an incredible assembly of believers gathered before the throne of God in heaven in Revelation 15...

And I saw another sign in heaven, great and marvellous, seven angels having the seven last plagues; for in them is filled up the wrath of God.

2 And I saw as it were a sea of glass mingled with fire: **and them that had gotten the victory over the beast, and over his image, and over his mark, and over the number of his name, stand on the sea of glass, having the harps of God.**

3 And they sing the song of Moses the servant of God, and the song of the Lamb, saying, Great and marvellous are thy works, Lord God Almighty; just and true are thy ways, thou King of saints.

4 Who shall not fear thee, O Lord, and glorify thy name? for thou only art holy: for all nations shall come and worship before thee; for thy judgments are made manifest.

Please note that this gathering of believers includes those "that had gotten the victory over the beast, and over his image, and over his mark, and over the number of his name".

So how did they get there?

In order to have "gotten the victory over the beast, and over his image, and over his mark, and over the number of his name", these believers would have had to have gone through the Tribulation period.

So how did they get to heaven?

Well, either they died or they were raptured. And since the rapture took place just one chapter earlier in Revelation 14, that would seem to be the most logical conclusion.

In Revelation 16, the vial judgments are poured out. Once again, I want to emphasize that there is absolutely no mention of believers being on Earth in this chapter. Personally, I believe that these vials are being poured out in rapid succession during the "Days of Awe" that stretch from the time we are raptured on the Feast of Trumpets (Rosh Hashanah) and when we triumphantly return with Jesus to this planet on Yom Kippur. I will break this down in much more detail in a future chapter.

In Revelation 17 and 18 there is a vision concerning the fall of Babylon the Great, and then in Revelation 19 we read about "the marriage of the Lamb" and "the marriage supper of the Lamb"...

*7 Let us be glad and rejoice, and give honour to him: for **the marriage of the Lamb** is come, and his wife hath made herself ready.*

8 And to her was granted that she should be arrayed in fine linen, clean and white: for the fine linen is the righteousness of saints.

*9 And he saith unto me, Write, Blessed are they which are called unto **the marriage supper of the Lamb**. And he saith unto me, These are the true sayings of God.*

If the Bride had already been raptured seven years earlier or three and a half years earlier, then why were the marriage of the Lamb and the marriage supper of the Lamb delayed for so long?

This is something that pre-Trib and mid-Trib "experts" really struggle with.

In ancient Israel, once a couple became engaged, the bridegroom would go to prepare a place for his bride. Once the father of the groom was satisfied that all of the preparations had been made, he would release his son to go gather his bride. Sometimes this would take place unexpectedly, and often in the middle of the night.

The groom would be accompanied by his friends as he made his way over to gather the bride, and often one of the friends would run ahead and blow a shofar to warn the bride that the groom was coming. I believe that this is a prophetic picture of the rapture of believers on Rosh Hashanah.

The wedding ceremony was usually held at the house of the groom's father, and after the ceremony there would be a feast for seven days.

I am convinced that we are seeing a similar pattern play out here at the end of the book of Revelation. We are raptured on the Feast of Trumpets (Rosh Hashanah) and we experience the marriage of the Lamb and the marriage supper of the Lamb within the 10 day period that stretches from Rosh Hashanah to Yom Kippur as the vials of God's wrath are poured out on Earth.

But after that, we rapidly transition into a time of war, and this is something that I will elaborate on in the next chapter...

-CHAPTER NINE-

The Battle Of Armageddon

For years, many have attempted to equate "the Battle of Armageddon" with some sort of nuclear showdown between global superpowers. And without a doubt, I do believe that World War III is coming and that nuclear weapons will be used. But the Battle of Armageddon has nothing to do with that. Rather, it is Satan's last ditch attempt to prevent the return of Jesus Christ to this planet.

In Revelation chapter 16, we read about the gathering of the armies of the entire world to a place in Israel known as "Armageddon". This comes just after the sixth vial is poured out. At this point, the forces of darkness realize that their time has come to an end and that the return of Jesus with the armies of heaven is imminent. So they gather together under the leadership of Satan, the Antichrist and the false prophet in order to try to repel this "invasion"...

12 And the sixth angel poured out his vial upon the great river Euphrates; and the water thereof was dried up, that the way of the kings of the east might be prepared.

13 And I saw three unclean spirits like frogs come out of the mouth of the dragon, and out of the mouth of the beast, and out of the mouth of the false prophet.

14 For they are the spirits of devils, working miracles, which go forth unto the kings of the earth and of the whole world, to gather them to the battle of that great day of God Almighty.

15 Behold, I come as a thief. Blessed is he that watcheth, and keepeth his garments, lest he walk naked, and they see his shame.

16 And he gathered them together into a place called in the Hebrew tongue Armageddon.

Of course this is a completely and totally futile effort. There is no way that they can possibly win, and yet they gather to fight against the Lord anyway.

In Revelation 19, we see the outcome of this great battle. Needless to say, it doesn't take long and the outcome is never in any doubt...

11 And I saw heaven opened, and behold a white horse; and he that sat upon him was called Faithful and True, and in righteousness he doth judge and make war.

12 His eyes were as a flame of fire, and on his head were many crowns; and he had a name written, that no man knew, but he himself.

13 And he was clothed with a vesture dipped in blood: and his name is called The Word of God.

14 And the armies which were in heaven followed him upon white horses, clothed in fine linen, white and clean.

15 And out of his mouth goeth a sharp sword, that with it he should smite the nations: and he shall rule them with a rod of iron: and he treadeth the winepress of the fierceness and wrath of Almighty God.

16 And he hath on his vesture and on his thigh a name written, King Of Kings, And Lord Of Lords.

17 And I saw an angel standing in the sun; and he cried with a loud voice, saying to all the fowls that fly in the midst of heaven, Come and gather yourselves together unto the supper of the great God;

18 That ye may eat the flesh of kings, and the flesh of captains, and the flesh of mighty men, and the flesh of horses, and of them that sit on them, and the flesh of all men, both free and bond, both small and great.

19 And I saw the beast, and the kings of the earth, and their armies, gathered together to make war against him that sat on the horse, and against his army.

20 And the beast was taken, and with him the false prophet that wrought miracles before him, with which he deceived them that had received the mark of the beast, and them that worshipped his image. These both were cast alive into a lake of fire burning with brimstone.

21 And the remnant were slain with the sword of him that sat upon the horse, which sword proceeded out of his mouth: and all the fowls were filled with their flesh.

A parallel passage in the Old Testament is found in Joel chapter 2. In this passage, we are told that the Lord will lead an indestructible conquering army back to Jerusalem at the coming of the Day of the Lord...

Blow ye the trumpet in Zion, and sound an alarm in my holy mountain: let all the inhabitants of the land tremble: ***for the day of the Lord cometh,*** *for it is nigh at hand;*

2 A day of darkness and of gloominess, a day of clouds and of thick darkness, as the morning spread upon the mountains: a great people and a strong; there hath not been ever the like, neither shall be any more after it, even to the years of many generations.

3 A fire devoureth before them; and behind them a flame burneth: the land is as the garden of Eden before them, and behind them a desolate wilderness; yea, and nothing shall escape them.

4 The appearance of them is as the appearance of horses; and as horsemen, so shall they run.

5 Like the noise of chariots on the tops of mountains shall they leap, like the noise of a flame of fire that devoureth the stubble, as a strong people set in battle array.

6 Before their face the people shall be much pained: all faces shall gather blackness.

7 They shall run like mighty men; they shall climb the wall like men of war; and they shall march every one on his ways, and they shall not break their ranks:

8 Neither shall one thrust another; they shall walk every one in his path: and when they fall upon the sword, they shall not be wounded.

9 They shall run to and fro in the city; they shall run upon the wall, they shall climb up upon the houses; they shall enter in at the windows like a thief.

10 **The earth shall quake before them; the heavens shall tremble: the sun and the moon shall be dark, and the stars shall withdraw their shining:**

11 And **the Lord shall utter his voice before his army***: for his camp is very great: for he is strong that executeth his word: for* **the day of the Lord** *is great and very terrible; and who can abide it?*

Can you see some of the parallels?

Jesus leads a great army on horses unlike anything the world has ever seen before, He defeats those that are trying to prevent his triumphant return to this planet, and the armies of heaven (which include those of us that believe in Him) will have a front row seat to the action.

In the Old Testament, they didn't use the term "the Millennial reign" to describe the coming 1000 year reign of the Messiah. Instead, we see other labels being used, and one of them is "the Day of the Lord". And there are multiple passages that tell us that "the coming of the Day of the Lord" will be a time of great chaos.

Another example of this can be found in Zechariah 14...

*Behold, **the day of the Lord cometh**, and thy spoil shall be divided in the midst of thee.*

2 For I will gather all nations against Jerusalem to battle; and the city shall be taken, and the houses rifled, and the women ravished; and half of the city shall go forth into captivity, and the residue of the people shall not be cut off from the city.

3 Then shall the Lord go forth, and fight against those nations, as when he fought in the day of battle.

*4 **And his feet shall stand in that day upon the mount of Olives**, which is before Jerusalem on the east, and the mount of Olives shall cleave in the midst thereof toward the east and toward the west, and there shall be a very great valley; and half of the mountain shall remove toward the north, and half of it toward the south.*

Take note that the place where the feet of Jesus first set down is on the Mount of Olives. This fulfills a promise that was made nearly two thousand years ago in Acts chapter 1...

7 And he said unto them, It is not for you to know the times or the seasons, which the Father hath put in his own power.

8 But ye shall receive power, after that the Holy Ghost is come upon you: and ye shall be witnesses unto me both in Jerusalem, and in all Judaea, and in Samaria, and unto the uttermost part of the earth.

9 And when he had spoken these things, while they beheld, he was taken up; and a cloud received him out of their sight.

10 And while they looked stedfastly toward heaven as he went up, behold, two men stood by them in white apparel;

*11 Which also said, Ye men of Galilee, why stand ye gazing up into heaven? this same Jesus, which is taken up from you into heaven, **shall so come in like manner as ye have seen him go into heaven**.*

*12 Then returned they unto Jerusalem **from the mount called Olivet**, which is from Jerusalem a sabbath day's journey.*

This tremendous battle brings to an end the reign of the Antichrist and humanity's six thousand year rebellion against God. After this great battle, our Lord and Savior Jesus Christ reigns over the whole world from Jerusalem for a thousand years.

There are many in the church world today that want to try to explain away the thousand year reign of Christ, but I don't see how they can possibly do that. If you read Revelation chapter 20, the term "thousand years" is used six different times.

You would think that would be enough times to convince the skeptics, but like I said earlier in this book, most people believe what they want to believe.

There is something else that I want to discuss in Revelation chapter 20 that is absolutely critical to our discussion. It is called "the First Resurrection", but I shall save that for the next chapter...

-CHAPTER TEN-

The First Resurrection

Most of those that believe in a pre-Tribulation rapture or a mid-Tribulation rapture don't like to refer to the rapture as "the resurrection", because it immediately points to all sorts of scriptural problems for their positions.

In Revelation 20, we read about two resurrections for humanity. The first resurrection is for believers, and it includes those "that were beheaded for the witness of Jesus, and for the word of God, and which had not worshipped the beast, neither his image, neither had received his mark upon their foreheads, or in their hands".

Now if there was a mass resurrection of believers at the beginning of the Tribulation period, how in the world could it include those "that were beheaded for the witness of Jesus, and for the word of God, and which had not worshipped the beast, neither his image, neither had received his mark upon their foreheads, or in their hands"?

That is a very good question, and it is one that many of the "experts" do not have a good answer for.

Here is that passage from Revelation chapter 20 in context...

And I saw an angel come down from heaven, having the key of the bottomless pit and a great chain in his hand.

2 And he laid hold on the dragon, that old serpent, which is the Devil, and Satan, and bound him a thousand years,

3 And cast him into the bottomless pit, and shut him up, and set a seal upon him, that he should deceive the nations no more, till the thousand years should be fulfilled: and after that he must be loosed a little season.

*4 And I saw thrones, and they sat upon them, and judgment was given unto them: and **I saw the souls of them that were beheaded for the witness of Jesus, and for the word of God, and which had not worshipped the beast, neither his image, neither had received his mark upon their foreheads, or in their hands**; and they lived and reigned with Christ a thousand years.*

*5 But the rest of the dead lived not again until the thousand years were finished. **This is the first resurrection**.*

6 Blessed and holy is he that hath part in the first resurrection: on such the second death hath no power, but they shall be priests of God and of Christ, and shall reign with him a thousand years.

We find a similar passage in Daniel chapter 12. It discusses an unprecedented time of trouble for the people of God followed by a resurrection of the dead...

*And at that time shall Michael stand up, the great prince which standeth for the children of thy people: **and there shall be a time of trouble**, such as never was since there was a nation even to that same time: and at that time thy people shall be delivered, every one that shall be found written in the book.*

*2 And **many of them that sleep in the dust of the earth shall awake**, some to everlasting life, and some to shame and everlasting contempt.*

3 And they that be wise shall shine as the brightness of the firmament; and they that turn many to righteousness as the stars for ever and ever.

So when does the rapture occur according to the book of Daniel?

Just like in the book of Revelation, the resurrection is placed after a time of great tribulation.

Nowhere in the Bible can you find a resurrection that comes before the Tribulation. In later chapters, we will deal with the passages that pre-Trib and mid-Trib "experts" use to justify their views, and we will see that under scrutiny they turn out to be exceedingly weak.

In a desperate attempt to salvage their pre-Trib or mid-Trib views, some of them are now pushing a theory that there will be multiple resurrections. But we just read in Revelation 20 that the resurrection at the end of the Tribulation period is referred to as "the First Resurrection".

What part of "first" do these people not understand?

Once again, I want to stress that God is not trying to trick us. When Jesus said that the rapture is "after the Tribulation", He meant what He said. And there is a reason why the Scriptures call the resurrection that comes at the end of the book of Revelation "the First Resurrection".

If we would just be willing to accept the plain meaning of the text of the Word of God we could have avoided decades of debate and controversy. Instead, confusion reigns rampant in the church, and millions of people are making major life decisions based on what the "theologians" are telling them.

The Bible is clear – there is only going to be one "rapture", and it is not going to happen at either the beginning or the middle of the Tribulation.

We will see more scriptural evidence for this in the next chapter...

-CHAPTER ELEVEN-

The Revealing Of The Man Of Sin

Did you know that the Bible specifically says that the Antichrist will be revealed **before** the rapture takes place? In 2 Thessalonians chapter 2, we are warned that certain things **must happen** before Jesus comes back and we are gathered to Him...

*Now we beseech you, brethren, **by the coming ("parousia") of our Lord Jesus Christ, and by our gathering together unto him,***

2 That ye be not soon shaken in mind, or be troubled, neither by spirit, nor by word, nor by letter as from us, as that the day of Christ is at hand.

*3 Let no man deceive you by any means: **for that day shall not come, except there come a falling away first, and that man of sin be revealed, the son of perdition;***

4 Who opposeth and exalteth himself above all that is called God, or that is worshipped; so that he as God sitteth in the temple of God, shewing himself that he is God.

5 Remember ye not, that, when I was yet with you, I told you these things?

The Apostle Paul was specifically instructing the believers in Thessalonica not to be troubled by those that were teaching that the day of Christ was at hand.

But isn't that precisely what we have seen for decades in churches in the western world? For years, there have be preachers running around proclaiming that "the rapture could happen tonight".

No, according to the Apostle Paul that simply is not accurate.

In verse one above, Paul states that he is talking about "the coming of our Lord Jesus Christ" and "our gathering together unto him".

When will that happen?

When will Jesus come and gather all believers to Himself?

Of course he is talking about the rapture. And in verse three, Paul says that there are some specific things to watch for before the rapture takes place.

First of all, we are told that there will be a great falling away. The Greek word used here is "apostasia". As you can guess, it is related to the English word "apostasy". And that is precisely what we are looking for. In these last days we should expect to see a great falling away or "apostasy" by those that call themselves Christians.

There are some pre-Trib scholars that would like to translate "apostasia" as "a catching away", but that doesn't make any sense at all. Firstly, there are never any instances where that Greek word is ever used in that manner, and secondly it ignores the clear context of the verse. It wouldn't make any sense for Paul to say that one of the signs that will happen before the rapture is the rapture.

No, clearly what is being taught here is that there will be a falling away by believers before the return of our Lord and Savior Jesus Christ.

So what might that falling away look like?

Well, many believe that it is related to the "strong delusion" that is mentioned later in the chapter...

11 And for this cause God shall send them strong delusion, that they should believe a lie:

12 That they all might be damned who believed not the truth, but had pleasure in unrighteousness.

There has been tremendous speculation over the years as to what that "strong delusion" might be, but the Scriptures are not more specific than this.

Personally, I wish that I could tell you exactly what it is, but I do not know. However, I am of the opinion that it will be something so extraordinary that it would be beyond what most of us would even have the capacity to imagine right now. It truly will be a "great delusion", and sadly millions of "believers" will fall for it.

Another thing that the Apostle Paul tells us must happen before the rapture is the revealing of the man of sin. In this passage in 2 Thessalonians, he is also referred to as "the son of perdition".

The Greek word that we find translated as "perdition" in our Bibles is "apoleia". We find that this exact same Greek word is also used twice in the book of Revelation to identify the Antichrist. The first instance is in Revelation 17:8...

*8 **The beast** that thou sawest was, and is not; and shall ascend out of the bottomless pit, and go into **perdition**: and they that dwell on the earth shall wonder, whose names were not written in the book of life from the foundation of the world, when they behold the beast that was, and is not, and yet is.*

The second instance is in Revelation 17:11...

*11 And **the beast** that was, and is not, even he is the eighth, and is of the seven, and goeth into **perdition**.*

So how will we know that someone is the Antichrist?

Well, the Apostle Paul tells us in this passage that this son of perdition will actually go into a rebuilt Jewish temple and proclaim himself to be God.

Therefore, we know that the temple of God will be rebuilt in Jerusalem in the last days and the Antichrist will go in and defile it before the rapture of believers takes place. And this fits exactly with what we read earlier in Matthew 24...

*15 When ye therefore shall see **the abomination of desolation**, spoken of by Daniel the prophet, stand in the holy place, (whoso readeth, let him understand:)*

16 Then let them which be in Judaea flee into the mountains:

17 Let him which is on the housetop not come down to take any thing out of his house:

18 Neither let him which is in the field return back to take his clothes.

19 And woe unto them that are with child, and to them that give suck in those days!

20 But pray ye that your flight be not in the winter, neither on the sabbath day:

*21 **For then shall be great tribulation**, such as was not since the beginning of the world to this time, no, nor ever shall be.*

2 Thessalonians chapter 2 and Matthew chapter 24 are [bo]th talking about the event that the prophet Daniel first described in Daniel chapter 9. This event is called "the abomination of desolation", and it involves the Antich[rist] going into the temple of God and proclaiming that he i[s] humanity's god.

In both 2 Thessalonians chapter 2 and Matthew chapt[er 2]4 we are told that this takes place before the rapture of t[he] church, and so this absolutely destroys all pre-Trib the[ori]es.

And as I noted earlier in this book, Matthew 24 explai[ns t]hat the abomination of desolation sets in motion a time of tribulation lasting three and a half years that will be so [gr]eat that Jesus tells us that there has never been a time like [it i]n all of human history nor shall there be a time like it eve[r] again. And then we are told that "after the tribulation [of] those days" Jesus is going to come get us.

That means that mid-Trib is out too.

If you don't take scriptures out of context and you let t[hem] all fit together like a puzzle, what the Bible is saying is actually exceedingly clear.

2 Thessalonians chapter 2 removes any argument for a [pr]e-Tribulation rapture, and it gives us specific events that [mu]st happen before the rapture will occur.

The reason why most Christians won't accept this teac[hin]g is because they don't want to accept it.

Most Christians in America today have been raised to [beli]eve that there will be a pre-Tribulation rapture, and they w[an]t to continue believing that.

I fear for those that are so hard-hearted that they cannot accept what the Bible plainly says.

When the "strong delusion" comes along, will they fall for that too?

-CHAPTER TWELVE-

The War Against The Saints

How can the Antichrist conduct a "war against the sain   if
all of the saints have already been taken away in a pre-
Tribulation rapture?

We have already seen that in Matthew 24 the abomina   ı of
desolation sets in motion three and a half years of grea
tribulation. In Revelation chapter 13, we are told that
Antichrist makes "war with the saints" during this time   nd
that he is able to overcome them. It will be a time of te   ng
for the church unlike anything that we have ever seen l   ıre.
In Revelation 13, this period of time is said to be 42 mc   ıs,
which works out to exactly three and a half years...

4 And they worshipped the dragon which gave power   *to*
the beast: and they worshipped the beast, saying, Wh
like unto the beast? who is able to make war with him

5 And there was given unto him a mouth speaking gre
things and blasphemies; and power was given unto h   *to*
*continue **forty and two months**.*

6 And he opened his mouth in blasphemy against God
blaspheme his name, and his tabernacle, and them th
dwell in heaven.

*7 And it was given unto him **to make war with the***
***saints**, and to overcome them: and power was given*   *n*
over all kindreds, and tongues, and nations.

8 And all that dwell upon the earth shall worship him
whose names are not written in the book of life of the   *nb*
slain from the foundation of the world.

9 If any man have an ear, let him hear.

10 He that leadeth into captivity shall go into captivity: he that killeth with the sword must be killed with the sword. **Here is the patience and the faith of the saints.**

But this is not the first time that this war on the saints is mentioned in the Scriptures. Several hundred years before John received this vision, the prophet Daniel was shown the same thing. We read the following in Daniel chapter 7...

15 I Daniel was grieved in my spirit in the midst of my body, and the visions of my head troubled me.

16 I came near unto one of them that stood by, and asked him the truth of all this. So he told me, and made me know the interpretation of the things.

17 These great beasts, which are four, are four kings, which shall arise out of the earth.

18 But the saints of the most High shall take the kingdom, and possess the kingdom for ever, even for ever and ever.

19 Then I would know the truth of the fourth beast, which was diverse from all the others, exceeding dreadful, whose teeth were of iron, and his nails of brass; which devoured, brake in pieces, and stamped the residue with his feet;

20 And of the ten horns that were in his head, and of the other which came up, and before whom three fell; even of that horn that had eyes, and a mouth that spake very great things, whose look was more stout than his fellows.

21 I beheld, and the same horn **made war with the saints**, *and prevailed against them;*

22 Until the Ancient of days came, and judgment was
to the saints of the most High; and the time came that
saints possessed the kingdom.

23 Thus he said, The fourth beast shall be the fourth
kingdom upon earth, which shall be diverse from all
kingdoms, and shall devour the whole earth, and shal
it down, and break it in pieces.

24 And the ten horns out of this kingdom are ten king
shall arise: and another shall rise after them; and he
be diverse from the first, and he shall subdue three kir

25 And he shall speak great words against the most H
and shall wear out the saints of the most High
think to change times and laws: **and they shall be**
into his hand until a time and times and the
dividing of time*.

26 But the judgment shall sit, and they shall take awa
dominion, to consume and to destroy it unto the end.

27 And the kingdom and dominion, and the greatness
kingdom under the whole heaven, shall be given to the
people of the saints of the most High, whose kingdom
everlasting kingdom, and all dominions shall serve a
obey him.

Once again, we see the exact same period of time ment
only here it is described as "a time, and times and the
dividing of time". For three and a half years the Antich
will "wear out the saints of the most High" and "they sl
given into his hand".

Is there any doubt that Daniel 7 and Revelation 13 are
about the exact same thing?

Of course not.

So why are there saints still running around to be persecuted?

Those that hold to a pre-Trib view or a mid-Trib view believe that all current believers have already been raptured at this point, and so they have come up with the term "Tribulation saints" to describe those that got "left behind" and quickly got saved afterwards once they realized the mistake that they made. So that is how they try to square their theories with what the Bible actually says.

But nowhere in the Bible is the term "Tribulation saints" ever used, and there is no mention of masses of people getting saved after a rapture event. This is a doctrine that theologians have made up completely out of thin air. Because they are convinced that their rapture theories must be true, they read things into the Scriptures that simply are not there.

Millions upon millions of Christians that are waiting for either a pre-Tribulation rapture or a mid-Tribulation rapture are going to end up having to face this "war against the saints", and they are going to be mentally, emotionally and spiritually unprepared for it because their preachers always taught them that they would never have to face it.

That is why we need to begin talking about the persecution that is coming to the church. It has already started in many areas around the globe, but in the western world we are still incredibly soft because we are used to having so much freedom. Sadly, this time of freedom is coming to an end, and things are about to become very rough for us as well.

When this great persecution comes, it has already got to be completely settled in our hearts and our minds that we are willing to die for what we believe.

I am completely convinced that we are the generation that will see the Mark of the Best implemented. If you and your family refuse to take it, you will be killed. If you and your family choose to accept it, you will live, but the end result will be far, far worse. We read the following in Revelation chapter 14...

9 And the third angel followed them, saying with a loud voice, If any man worship the beast and his image, and receive his mark in his forehead, or in his hand,

10 The same shall drink of the wine of the wrath of God, which is poured out without mixture into the cup of his indignation; and he shall be tormented with fire and brimstone in the presence of the holy angels, and in the presence of the Lamb:

11 And the smoke of their torment ascendeth up for ever and ever: and they have no rest day nor night, who worship the beast and his image, and whosoever receiveth the mark of his name.

Could it be possible that some Christians will ultimately take the Mark of the Beast because they don't recognize what is happening because they always expected a rapture to come before the Mark of the Beast is unveiled?

Let's hope not.

And there may be many believers that lose their faith completely once they realize that the pre-Tribulation rapture is a lie. Since the pre-Tribulation rapture is so central to the faith of so many, the crumbling of that doctrine may cause many to turn away from the faith altogether.

These are just some of the reasons why we need to tell people the truth. The Bible tells us what to expect so that we will not be afraid. Yes, times are going to be incredibly challenging, but God is in control and He has a plan.

And there are a lot worse things than death. For those of us that know Jesus, death is simply a doorway into eternity. Because we know Him, we have been given the ultimate happy ending. We are going to spend forever with our Savior in a place where there is no longer any suffering or pain or death.

So we can face the future without fear. The worst that the enemy can do is kill us, and all that is going to do is send us home.

Revelation 12:11 tells us how we will get the victory…

11 And they overcame him by the blood of the Lamb, and by the word of their testimony; and they loved not their lives unto the death.

The Bible tells us that the Antichrist is going to unleash the greatest wave of Christian persecution the world has ever seen. But in the process we are going to bring glory to our Lord and Savior, and we are going to bring in the greatest harvest of souls the world has ever seen.

The Scriptures also tell us about a place of refuge where large numbers of believers will be kept safe during this time, and I am going to talk about that extensively in a later chapter.

But for now I want to stress that whatever our fate, each one of us has already got to be willing to die for Jesus without any hesitation. There is simply no other way to face what is coming.

We have got to be bold, we have got to be fearless, and we have got to be recklessly in love with Him.

A great war on the saints is coming, but it is not something to be feared.

In fact, I believe that it will be one of the greatest hours the church has ever known.

-CHAPTER THIRTEEN-

God Has A Calendar

God has a calendar, and it is very different from our calendar. I had been going to church for decades before I ever learned anything about this. But now after years of intensive research, I am fully convinced that it is incredibly difficult to have even an elementary understanding of Bible prophecy unless you first understand the Biblical calendar.

Earlier in this book I mentioned Biblical festivals such as Rosh Hashanah and Yom Kippur, and we will explore them some more in just a little bit, but let's start with the basics. At the creation of the world, God created the sun and the moon and the stars, and in Genesis chapter 1 we read that he intended them to be "for signs" and "for seasons"...

14 And God said, Let there be lights in the firmament of the heaven to divide the day from the night; and let them be for signs, and for seasons, and for days, and years

And on a very basic level, this has definitely turned out to be the case. For example, the length of our day is based on the rotation of our planet in relation to the sun.

Similarly, in ancient cultures the length of a month was determined based on the position of the moon. In ancient Israel, God instructed the people to celebrate each "new moon", and this is still practiced by many believers around the world today.

The length of our week is based on the length of time that it took God to create the world. The Bible tells us that He created all things in six days and that on the seventh day He rested. We read the following in Genesis chapter 2...

2 And on the seventh day God ended his work which he had made; and he rested on the seventh day from all his work which he had made.

3 And God blessed the seventh day, and sanctified it: because that in it he had rested from all his work which God created and made.

All of God's holy days involve looking back and remembering something that He has done. On the seventh day of the week we are commanded to rest and remember Him as our Creator. Could the fact that we are not doing this be a significant factor in why our society has rejected Him as Creator and instead has chosen to embrace the fairytale of Darwinian evolution?

That is certainly something to think about.

Also, if God made the seventh day of the week holy at the very creation of the world, when did it become unholy?

A lot of people want to try to claim that the Sabbath does not exist anymore, but the Bible says otherwise. In Isaiah chapter 66, the Word of God tells us that the Sabbath will remain forever, even after the new heavens and the new earth have been created...

22 For as the new heavens and the new earth, which I will make, shall remain before me, saith the Lord, so shall your seed and your name remain.

23 And it shall come to pass, that from one new moon to another, and from one sabbath to another, shall all flesh come to worship before me, saith the Lord.

In addition to the weekly Sabbath, God instituted a number of other important festivals that fall throughout the year.

We just read Genesis 1:14 above, and the Hebrew word used for "seasons" in that verse is Strong's H4150. In English, we would pronounce it "mow-ed" or "mo-ade". It means "appointed time" or "appointed meeting" and it is the exact same word that is translated as "feasts" in Leviticus chapter 23.

In Leviticus 23 and elsewhere throughout the Torah, we read about "the feasts of the Lord". As I noted above, God's days are always about remembering something, but they are also about looking forward to what is to come. Pastor Mark Biltz of El Shaddai Ministries has described them as "dress rehearsals", and I think that is very accurate. All of these appointed times are ultimately about Jesus, and they all highlight different aspects of His ministry.

For example, let's take a few moments to look at how the first coming of Jesus fulfilled the spring feasts to the very day.

Did you know that for centuries ahead of time, God held a "dress rehearsal" for the crucifixion of Jesus the Messiah every single year in the exact city where it would happen and on the exact day when it would happen? It is called Pesach (Passover), and it is greatly misunderstood. Even though this day is all about Jesus the Messiah, most of the people who celebrate it don't even believe in Jesus. And most of the people that believe in Jesus don't celebrate it. But as you will see below, the Scriptures have some amazing things to say about Passover.

In 1 Corinthians 5:7-8, we are told that Jesus is our Passover lamb…

7 Purge out therefore the old leaven, that ye may be a new lump, as ye are unleavened. For even Christ our passover is sacrificed for us:

8 Therefore let us keep the feast, not with old leaven, neither with the leaven of malice and wickedness; but with the unleavened bread of sincerity and truth.

On Passover, the people of Israel are commanded to gather in Jerusalem to remember the exodus out of the land of Egypt.

During the original Passover, right before the people of Israel left Egypt, God instructed the people of Israel to kill a lamb and to put the blood of that lamb on the doorposts so that the death angel would pass over their homes. Because Pharaoh would not let the people of Israel go, God sent a plague which killed all of the firstborn sons, but those who had their doorposts covered by the blood of a lamb were spared from the plague. It was a time of great deliverance for the people of Israel that we remember down to this day.

So why did God have His people put the blood of a lamb on their doorposts?

Why be that specific?

Well, even today most doorposts are made out of wood.

And where does wood come from?

It comes from a tree.

So the message of the original Passover was that the blood of the lamb on the tree delivered them from the wrath of God.

And that foreshadowed precisely what would happen on that day more than 1000 years later, and it is the very heart of the gospel message.

After the people of Israel got to the Promised Land, God required that His people gather in Jerusalem on that specific day every single year in order to celebrate the Passover.

Looking back, we can now see that God had His people gather together every single year in the exact city where Jesus would die, on the exact day when Jesus would die, and He had them act out rituals which precisely foreshadowed the shedding of the blood of the lamb on the tree (the cross).

Even though this was done every single year for centuries in advance, most of the people still missed it.

And the parallels between Jesus the Messiah and the Passover lamb are astonishing.

First of all, both Jesus and the Passover lamb were males and were "without blemish".

Secondly, the bones of the Passover lamb were not to be broken, and the bones of Jesus were not broken on the cross either even though it was customary to break the legs of those being crucified to speed up their deaths.

Thirdly, the Passover lamb was always bound to the altar at 9 AM. That is precisely the time when the Scriptures tell us that Jesus was nailed to the cross.

Fourthly, the Passover lamb was always sacrificed at 3 PM. At that moment, a priest would blow a shofar at the Temple and the people would quietly contemplate what had just happened. That is precisely the time when the Scriptures tell us that Jesus declared "It is finished" and died on the cross. The veil of the Temple was supernaturally torn from top to bottom, and there was a great earthquake. The lamb of God paid for our sins, just as the day of Passover had been foreshadowing for more than 1000 years.

Immediately after Passover is the Feast of Unleavened Bread. In Exodus 12:15, we are told that during this festival we are to put away all leaven out of our houses...

Seven days shall ye eat unleavened bread; even the first day ye shall put away leaven out of your houses: for whosoever eateth leavened bread from the first day until the seventh day, that soul shall be cut off from Israel.

So why would God have us do such a thing?

Well, in the Scriptures leaven always represents sin.

We remove leaven from our homes to show that the lamb of God removed all of our sin on Passover.

It is a perfect picture of what Jesus has done for us.

During the week of the Feast of Unleavened Bread, a very special celebration known as "Firstfruits" takes place. Once again, this is a day that is pointing to Jesus. In fact, in 1 Corinthians 15 Christ is even specifically referred to as "the firstfruits"...

*20 But now is Christ risen from the dead, and become **the firstfruits** of them that slept.*

21 For since by man came death, by man came also the resurrection of the dead.

22 For as in Adam all die, even so in Christ shall all be made alive.

23 But every man in his own order: Christ the firstfruits; afterward they that are Christ's at his coming.

Did you know that for centuries ahead of time, God held a "dress rehearsal" for the resurrection of Jesus the Messiah every single year in the exact city where it would happen and on the exact day that it would happen?

During the Festival of Unleavened Bread, the day after the regular weekly Sabbath that falls during those seven days is known as Firstfruits. The people of Israel would bring "a sheaf of the firstfruits" to the high priest who would wave it before the Lord. By doing so, the people of Israel were signifying that they trusted in the Lord to bring in the rest of the harvest.

Well, in the Scriptures the Apostle Paul describes Jesus the Messiah as "the firstfruits" of those that would rise from the dead. And we trust that at His coming the rest of the harvest will be bodily resurrected at that time as well. The Scriptures promise us that not only will our spirits live forever, but that our actual physical bodies will be resurrected someday too.

In 1 Corinthians 15:51-52 we read the following...

51 Behold, I shew you a mystery; We shall not all sleep, but we shall all be changed,

52 In a moment, in the twinkling of an eye, at the last trump: for the trumpet shall sound, and the dead shall be raised incorruptible, and we shall be changed.

I referenced that passage earlier in this book, and it is a description of the rapture.

After reading what you have read so far, would it surprise you to know that there is another Biblical festival that specifically foreshadows the rapture?

This is something that I will discuss in the next chapter...

-CHAPTER FOURTEEN-

The Dress Rehearsal For The Rapture

Very few people out there have any idea that there is a very strong link between the Biblical festival of Rosh Hashanah and the rapture. Millions of Jews celebrate this holiday every year without even understanding that it is all about Jesus, and most Christians don't pay any attention to it at all.

But even though it is greatly misunderstood, God has big plans for this festival. The truth is that there is a reason why God commands that the shofar be blown on Rosh Hashanah – it is because the blast of the trumpet is connected to the ultimate prophetic fulfillment of this holiday.

You see, God almost always does the "big things" on His festival days. Jesus was crucified on Passover, He was in the grave on the first day of the Feast of Unleavened Bread, He was raised from the dead on First Fruits, and the Holy Spirit was poured out on the first believers during the Feast of Pentecost.

Every single one of the Biblical festivals is prophetic.

So what is prophetic about Rosh Hashanah and the blowing of the shofar?

Well, there are several primary scriptures that describe the return of Jesus to this earth, and in those scriptures a blast from a trumpet repeatedly shows up.

For example, let's recall what 1 Corinthians 15 says...

51 Behold, I shew you a mystery; We shall not all sleep, but we shall all be changed,

*52 In a moment, in the twinkling of an eye, **at the last trump**: for the trumpet shall sound, and the dead shall be raised incorruptible, and we shall be changed.*

53 For this corruptible must put on incorruption, and this mortal must put on immortality.

54 So when this corruptible shall have put on incorruption, and this mortal shall have put on immortality, then shall be brought to pass the saying that is written, Death is swallowed up in victory.

55 O death, where is thy sting? O grave, where is thy victory?

This passage tells us that the second coming of Jesus will take place at the last trumpet.

So when will that be?

Well, hold on to that thought for a minute and let's take a look at the next passage.

In 1 Thessalonians 4, once again we see that the timing of the rapture coincides with the trumpet call of God...

14 For if we believe that Jesus died and rose again, even so them also which sleep in Jesus will God bring with him.

15 For this we say unto you by the word of the Lord, that we which are alive and remain unto the coming of the Lord shall not prevent them which are asleep.

*16 For the Lord himself shall descend from heaven with a shout, with the voice of the archangel, **and with the trump of God**: and the dead in Christ shall rise first:*

17 Then we which are alive and remain shall be ught up together with them in the clouds, to meet the Lo n the air: and so shall we ever be with the Lord.

There is that trumpet again.

Is God putting that in there to confuse us?

Of course not. There is a reason why the blowing a trumpet keeps showing up. God wants us to kno hat all of these various passages are describing the exact s e thing.

In Matthew chapter 24, Jesus tells His disciples ut many of the events that will occur during the Tribulatic period, and then in verses 29 to 31 Jesus describes the m ent of the rapture at the end of the Tribulation period. ase notice that once again, the events of Matthew 24 -31 coincide with the trumpet call of God...

29 Immediately after the tribulation of those da hall the sun be darkened, and the moon shall not give he ght, and the stars shall fall from heaven, and the powers the heavens shall be shaken:

30 And then shall appear the sign of the Son of i n in heaven: and then shall all the tribes of the earth urn, and they shall see the Son of man coming in the clou f heaven with power and great glory.

*31 And he shall send his angels **with a great s d of a trumpet**, and they shall gather together his ele rom the four winds, from one end of heaven to the other.*

I know that I am being a bit repetitive, but I am (g it for a reason.

The people of God have been celebrating a holiday known as "the Feast of Trumpets" every single year for thousands of years, and it is foreshadowing one of the most dramatic moments in human history that will involve the blowing of a trumpet.

Once you grasp this, it all seems so simple. In fact, you will kick yourself for not seeing it earlier.

The reality is that I Corinthians 15, 1 Thessalonians 4 and Matthew 24 are all talking about the exact same event – the rapture at the blowing of the last trumpet. Just like with every other major event in the ministry of Jesus, this event is specifically foreshadowed by the Biblical festivals.

But most Christians don't understand these things today, because unlike the early church, most churches don't celebrate the Feast of Trumpets anymore.

We have been given this amazing "dress rehearsal" which looks forward to the day when we will be gathered to our Savior, and yet very few people are even interested in celebrating it. And most of the Jewish people that do celebrate it don't understand what it actually means.

The Feast of Trumpets has also been known since ancient times as "the Hidden Feast". The reason it is called this is because in ancient times nobody ever quite knew when it was going to begin. The Feast of Trumpets falls on the first day of the seventh month on the Hebrew calendar, but the new month could not begin until the new moon was spotted. Once the new moon was finally spotted, then the Feast of Trumpets could officially commence. That is why even today the Jewish people allocate two days for the celebration of this festival.

The phrase "no man knows the day or the hour" ; commonly used to refer to this festival in ancient rael. So when Jesus used this phrase, He was pointing us this holiday. This is something that I am going to cov more extensively in a future chapter.

Just as the spring festivals were fulfilled to the ve day by the first coming of Jesus, so I believe that the fall stivals will be fulfilled to the very day by the second com ; of Jesus.

In some future year on Rosh Hashanah, a great t npet will blow and we will be taken home. This will happe n the day immediately after the seven year Tribulation peri has ended, and it will usher in the "Ten Days of Awe' tring which the wrath of God will be poured out in the l judgments. It will essentially be God's version of nock and awe". At the end of those ten days we will return th Jesus to this planet on Yom Kippur for the Battle of Ar geddon, and that is going to be the topic of my next chapt .

-CHAPTER FIFTEEN-

Yom Kippur, The Return Of Jesus & The Book Of Joel

In the last couple of chapters we have discussed how each of the Biblical festivals foreshadow key events in the ministry of Jesus, and at the end of the last chapter I expressed my belief that the blowing of "the last trumpet" will happen on Rosh Hashanah (the Feast of Trumpets).

In this chapter, we are going to examine the potential future fulfillment of Yom Kippur (the Day of Atonement).

God instructed the people of Israel to observe Yom Kippur on the 10th day of the 7th month of the Israelite calendar. Even today, it is regarded by the Jews as the most solemn day of the year. On that day the people of Israel were instructed to "afflict their souls" (humble themselves and fast) and it was the only day of the entire year in which the High Priest could enter into the Holy of Holies.

In Leviticus 23:26-32, we read what the people of Israel were instructed to do on that day...

26 And the Lord spake unto Moses, saying,

27 Also on the tenth day of this seventh month there shall be a day of atonement: it shall be an holy convocation unto you; and ye shall afflict your souls, and offer an offering made by fire unto the Lord.

28 And ye shall do no work in that same day: for it is a day of atonement, to make an atonement for you before the Lord your God.

*29 For whatsoever soul it be that shall not be aff   ed in
that same day, he shall be cut off from among h   eople.*

*30 And whatsoever soul it be that doeth any wo   n that
same day, the same soul will I destroy from am(his
people.*

*31 Ye shall do no manner of work: it shall be a s   ute for
ever throughout your generations in all your du   ings.*

*32 It shall be unto you a sabbath of rest, and ye   ll afflict
your souls: in the ninth day of the month at ever   om even
unto even, shall ye celebrate your sabbath.*

In Leviticus 16, the Scriptures describe for us the   ties of
the High Priest during the time of Yom Kippur, a   in
Hebrews 9:24-28 we are taught that Jesus is now   ir High
Priest and that He fulfilled what Yom Kippur hac
foreshadowed for so many generations...

*24 For Christ is not entered into the holy places   de with
hands, which are the figures of the true; but intc   aven
itself, now to appear in the presence of God for ι*

*25 Nor yet that he should offer himself often, as   high
priest entereth into the holy place every year wi   blood of
others;*

*26 For then must he often have suffered since th
foundation of the world: but now once in the en(f the
world hath he appeared to put away sin by the s   rifice of
himself.*

*27 And as it is appointed unto men once to die, l   after this
the judgment:*

28 So Christ was once offered to bear the sins of many; and unto them that look for him shall he appear the second time without sin unto salvation.

As I mentioned in the last chapter, I also believe that Yom Kippur will be the day when Jesus returns with His army, defeats the forces of the Antichrist, and sets down on the Mount of Olives.

Before Jesus even came the first time, this event was prophesied in the book of Zechariah. In Zechariah 14:1-4, we read the following...

*Behold, **the day of the Lord cometh**, and thy spoil shall be divided in the midst of thee.*

2 For I will gather all nations against Jerusalem to battle; and the city shall be taken, and the houses rifled, and the women ravished; and half of the city shall go forth into captivity, and the residue of the people shall not be cut off from the city.

3 Then shall the Lord go forth, and fight against those nations, as when he fought in the day of battle.

*4 **And his feet shall stand in that day upon the mount of Olives**, which is before Jerusalem on the east, and the mount of Olives shall cleave in the midst thereof toward the east and toward the west, and there shall be a very great valley; and half of the mountain shall remove toward the north, and half of it toward the south.*

In this passage in Zechariah, we are told that this occurs at the coming of "the day of the Lord". Another Old Testament prophet that spoke of the same thing was the prophet Joel, and his description of the coming of the Day of the Lord seems to link this event directly with Yom Kippur.

Joel 1:14-15 says the following...

*14 Sanctify ye **a fast**, call **a solemn assembly** ather the elders and all the inhabitants of the land into the ouse of the Lord your God, and cry unto the Lord,*

*15 Alas for the day! **for the day of the Lord is** t hand, and as a destruction from the Almighty shall it c e.*

Please note that in verse 15 the exact same phras the day of the Lord", that we saw in Zechariah 14 is used ce again.

But in this instance there are instructions to sanc a fast and "call a solemn assembly".

Well, a solemn assembly could refer to any of the stival days, but there is only one on which the people o rael were commanded to fast – Yom Kippur.

In case we missed it the first time, we see a simil assage in Joel chapter 2. These verses that I am about to s e with you come immediately after the first 11 verses of l 2 which we studied earlier in this book...

*12 Therefore also now, saith the Lord, turn ye e to me with all your heart, and with **fasting**, and with eping, and with mourning:*

13 And rend your heart, and not your garments, and turn unto the Lord your God: for he is gracious and merciful, slow to anger, and of great kindness, and repenteth him of the evil.

14 Who knoweth if he will return and repent, and leave a blessing behind him; even a meat offering and a drink offering unto the Lord your God?

*15 Blow the trumpet in Zion, sanctify **a fast**, call **a solemn assembly**:*

16 Gather the people, sanctify the congregation, assemble the elders, gather the children, and those that suck the breasts: let the bridegroom go forth of his chamber, and the bride out of her closet.

Once again we see instructions to fast and a call for a solemn assembly.

Do you think that this is just a coincidence?

Yom Kippur is the only day on the Biblical calendar when we are commanded to fast and hold a solemn assembly on the same day. I don't think that it is any accident that Joel repeated these details more than once in his passages about the coming of the Day of the Lord.

We are also told by Joel that it is a time when the bridegroom and the bride will leave their chambers.

So why is that significant?

Well, in Revelation 19:7-9, we are told that the marriage of the Lamb occurs just before the glorious return of Jesus to this planet...

7 Let us be glad and rejoice, and give honour to him: for the marriage of the Lamb is come, and his wife hath made herself ready.

*8 And to her was granted that she should be arrayed **in fine linen, clean and white**: for the fine linen is the righteousness of saints.*

9 And he saith unto me, Write, Blessed are they which are called unto the marriage supper of the Lamb. And he saith unto me, These are the true sayings of God.

After the marriage celebration in Revelation 19, we quickly switch to a war footing later on in that same chapter when we return with Jesus for the Battle of Armageddon.

And please take special note of the "fine linen, clean and white" mentioned in this passage.

Even today, many Jewish men wear a white robe-like garment called a "kittel" on Yom Kippur. In fact, this garment is used by some Orthodox males on their wedding day.

Not only that, but when the Temple was still standing, on Yom Kippur the High Priest would change into special white linen garments at one point during the ceremonies of the day.

In addition, it is important to note that it has been customary for centuries for all Jewish people to dress in white on Yom Kippur.

So the fact that the saints are given "fine linen, clean and white" to wear on that day may be a little more prophetic than we may have realized.

In fact, in Revelation 19:14 this fine linen is mentioned once again...

*14 And the armies which were in heaven followed him upon white horses, **clothed in fine linen, white and clean**.*

Another detail from Revelation 19 to take note of is found in verse 13....

13 And he was clothed with a vesture dipped in blood: and his name is called The Word of God.

Blood was a key feature of the celebration of Yom Kippur. It was the one day during the year when the High Priest could enter into the Holy Of Holies. The High Priest would take the blood from the bull that had been sacrificed and would sprinkle it on the mercy seat.

In Revelation 19, Jesus returns in a robe that has been dipped in blood, signifying that He was the true atonement for our sins.

Going back to the book of Joel, I am fully convinced that the entire book is a parallel account of the return of Jesus Christ with His army that we find in Revelation chapter 19. Just compare the two passages. First, here are the first eleven verses of Joel 2...

Blow ye the trumpet in Zion, and sound an alarm in my holy mountain: let all the inhabitants of the land tremble: for the day of the Lord cometh, for it is nigh at hand;

2 A day of darkness and of gloominess, a day of clouds and of thick darkness, as the morning spread upon the mountains: a great people and a strong; there hath not been ever the like, neither shall be any more after it, even to the years of many generations.

3 A fire devoureth before them; and behind them a flame burneth: the land is as the garden of Eden before them, and behind them a desolate wilderness; yea, and nothing shall escape them.

4 The appearance of them is as the appearance of horses; and as horsemen, so shall they run.

5 Like the noise of chariots on the tops of mountains shall they leap, like the noise of a flame of fire that devoureth the stubble, as a strong people set in battle array.

6 Before their face the people shall be much pained: all faces shall gather blackness.

7 They shall run like mighty men; they shall climb the wall like men of war; and they shall march every one on his ways, and they shall not break their ranks:

8 Neither shall one thrust another; they shall walk every one in his path: and when they fall upon the sword, they shall not be wounded.

9 They shall run to and fro in the city; they shall run upon the wall, they shall climb up upon the houses; they shall enter in at the windows like a thief.

10 The earth shall quake before them; the heavens shall tremble: the sun and the moon shall be dark, and the stars shall withdraw their shining:

11 And the Lord shall utter his voice before his army: for his camp is very great: for he is strong that executeth his word: for the day of the Lord is great and very terrible; and who can abide it?

Now, compare that with Revelation 19:11-21...

11 And I saw heaven opened, and behold a white horse; and he that sat upon him was called Faithful and True, and in righteousness he doth judge and make war.

12 His eyes were as a flame of fire, and on his head were many crowns; and he had a name written, that no man knew, but he himself.

13 And he was clothed with a vesture dipped in blood: and his name is called The Word of God.

14 And the armies which were in heaven followed him upon white horses, clothed in fine linen, white and clean.

15 And out of his mouth goeth a sharp sword, that with it he should smite the nations: and he shall rule them with a rod of iron: and he treadeth the winepress of the fierceness and wrath of Almighty God.

16 And he hath on his vesture and on his thigh a name written, King Of Kings, And Lord Of Lords.

17 And I saw an angel standing in the sun; and he cried with a loud voice, saying to all the fowls that fly in the midst of heaven, Come and gather yourselves together unto the supper of the great God;

18 That ye may eat the flesh of kings, and the flesh of captains, and the flesh of mighty men, and the flesh of horses, and of them that sit on them, and the flesh of all men, both free and bond, both small and great.

19 And I saw the beast, and the kings of the earth, and their armies, gathered together to make war against him that sat on the horse, and against his army.

20 And the beast was taken, and with him the false prophet that wrought miracles before him, with which he deceived them that had received the mark of the beast, and them that worshipped his image. These both were cast alive into a lake of fire burning with brimstone.

21 And the remnant were slain with the sword of him that sat upon the horse, which sword proceeded out of his mouth: and all the fowls were filled with their flesh.

In both instances, we see the Lord leading a m[igh]ty, unbeatable army on horses that is completely [vict]orious over the enemy.

I believe that both passages are describing the [exa]ct same event – the return of Jesus Christ at the Battle [of] Armageddon on the Day of Atonement (Yom K[ipp]ur).

A few days after Yom Kippur, the Feast of Tab[ern]acles begins.

The Feast of Tabernacles is a time of great rejo[icin]g, and the theme of the festival can be described as "God [dw]elling with man". The Feast of Tabernacles was when the [glo]ry of God visibly filled the first Temple as it was dedicate[d b]y Solomon following the completion of its construction (2 [Ch]ronicles 7), many believe that Jesus was born during the F[eas]t of Tabernacles, and I am convinced that it will be [a t]ime of great celebration when Jesus takes His place o[n th]e throne in Jerusalem (Ezekiel 43) to rule over this world [for] a thousand years (Revelation 20). In fact, Zechariah 14 sp[eci]fically mentions the fact that Jesus will require the w[hol]e world to celebrate the Feast of Tabernacles once He ret[urn]s...

16 And it shall come to pass, that every one th[at i]s left of all the nations which came against Jerusalem sh[all] even go up from year to year to worship the King, the Lo[rd] of hosts, and **to keep the feast of tabernacles.**

17 And it shall be, that whoso will not come u[p of] all the families of the earth unto Jerusalem to worsh[ip] the King, the Lord of hosts, even upon them shall be no [rai]n.

18 And if the family of Egypt go not up, and c[ome] not, that have no rain; there shall be the plague, where[wit]h the Lord *will smite the heathen **that come not up to keep the feast of tabernacles**.*

*19 This shall be the punishment of Egypt, and the punishment of all nations **that come not up to keep the feast of tabernacles**.*

Do you see what is being said here?

During the Millennial Kingdom, those that do not go up to Jerusalem to worship Jesus and celebrate the Feast of Tabernacles will be punished with no rain.

So everyone better get used to observing the Feast of Tabernacles, because when Jesus comes back it is going to be standard operating procedure.

But most Christians have never heard anything about this because their churches are not teaching them these things.

Like I said earlier, unless you understand the Biblical calendar it is going to be very difficult for you to truly understand much about Bible prophecy.

God is working off of a calendar that He established at the very beginning, and it has a whole lot to say about the very end.

If this is the first time that you have encountered this material, I understand that it may be quite confusing. If you have any questions about this or anything else, please feel free to reach out to me using the contact information at the end of this book.

-CHAPTER SIXTEEN-

We Are Not Appointed To Wrath

Those that believe in a pre-Tribulation rapture cannot show you where it says that there will be a rapture before the Tribulation begins in the Bible, so they have to resort to pulling scriptures out of context in order to make their points.

One of the favorite arguments that pre-Tribbers like to make is that since we "are not appointed to wrath" that it is impossible for us to go through the Tribulation period.

On the surface that sounds somewhat logical. Since we "are not appointed to wrath", we have got to get pulled out of here before anything bad happens, right?

Wrong.

The verse where it says that we are not appointed to wrath comes from 1 Thessalonians chapter 5, and it is not talking about the Tribulation period. Instead, it is all about personal salvation. Here is what 1 Thessalonians 5:9-10 actually says...

9 For God hath not appointed us to wrath, but to obtain salvation by our Lord Jesus Christ,

10 Who died for us, that, whether we wake or sleep, we should live together with him.

This passage is simply telling us that we have been saved through faith in Jesus Christ and that we are not going to hell. To try to extend the meaning of this passage into a doctrine that says that nothing bad will ever happen to us is absolutely ridiculous, and it is a grave mishandling of the Word of God.

What is being said in 1 Thessalonians 5 is essentially the exact same thing that is being said in John 3:36...

36 He that believeth on the Son hath everlasting life: and he that believeth not the Son shall not see life; but the wrath of God abideth on him.

The Bible never promises us that God will never punish believers. In fact, in 1 Peter 4:17 my Bible says that judgment actually begins with the house of God...

*17 For the time is come **that judgment must begin at the house of God**: and if it first begin at us, what shall the end be of them that obey not the gospel of God?*

The truth is that we see God coming down on His people all throughout the Scriptures. It happened again and again to the people of Israel as they wandered around in the wilderness before entering the promised land, in the book of Acts we see Ananias and Sapphira being struck dead for lying, and in Revelation chapters 2 and 3 we see Jesus warning about all sorts of consequences for churches that won't repent and get right with Him.

This notion that believers today will never have to face any difficulties before they are suddenly pulled out of here is very much a western phenomenon. In places like China, India and the Middle East, believers have to face trials and persecution on a daily basis.

Is it because they are inferior to us? Of course not!

In war-torn countries like Iraq and Syria, large numbers of believers are being crucified and beheaded by ISIS.

Where was their rapture?

The Bible never promises that Christians will escape tribulation. In fact, in John 16:33 we are promised that we **will** have tribulation...

*33 These things I have spoken unto you, that in me ye might have peace. In the world **ye shall have tribulation**: but be of good cheer; I have overcome the world.*

Millions of believers in the western world are going to be absolutely stunned when they realize that they have entered the Tribulation period and no rapture has happened yet.

They won't understand what is happening, because they were assured that they "were not appointed to wrath."

But just like believers all throughout history, we're going to have to go through trials too, and 1 Peter 4 says that we should not consider this to be a strange thing..

*12 Beloved, **think it not strange** concerning the fiery trial which is to try you, as though some strange thing happened unto you:*

13 But rejoice, inasmuch as ye are partakers of Christ's sufferings; that, when his glory shall be revealed, ye may be glad also with exceeding joy.

On top of everything else that I have written in this chapter, it is important to remember that the full measure of the wrath of God is not poured out until after the rapture anyway.

If you will recall, the rapture takes place in Revelation 14 before any of the vial judgments are poured out. In Revelation 15:7, we are told that the "seven golden vials" are "full of the wrath of God". These seven vials are poured out during the Days of Awe which stretch from when we are raptured (Rosh Hashanah) to the return of Jesus Christ with His army on Yom Kippur.

Yes, we are not going to be around for those judgments, but in Matthew 24 Jesus specifically warns us that we are going to have to endure a period of great tribulation "such as was not since the beginning of the world to this time, no, nor ever shall be".

So we are going to need to take off the training diapers and start seeking God like never before, because without His help there is no way that we are going to be able to face what is ahead.

Those Christians that are sitting at home on their sofas eating chips and watching television as they wait for their helicopter ride out of here are going to be deeply and bitterly disappointed.

And they certainly will not be physically, mentally, emotionally or spiritually prepared for what is ahead of them.

Hopefully this book will help wake some of them up, because right now most of the church in America is dead asleep and time is rapidly running out.

-CHAPTER SEVENTEEN-

Pray That You May Escape

Many of those that believe in a pre-Tribulation rapture refer to it as "the blessed hope", because they are hoping like crazy to get out of here before anything really bad starts happening. Sadly, I personally know quite a few pre-Tribbers that have already checked out on life. They have believed that the rapture is "imminent" for so long that they have never bothered to plan for the future or attempt great things for God. It is a Christian form of "escapism" that is extremely dangerous.

What I am going to share in this chapter is similar to what I talked about in the last chapter, but I felt that it needed to be addressed by itself.

One of the most popular verses that pre-Tribbers like to use is Luke 21:36...

36 Watch ye therefore, and pray always, that ye may be accounted worthy to escape all these things that shall come to pass, and to stand before the Son of man.

It is a wonderful, dramatic verse that pre-Trib preachers like to belt out all over the land during their sermons.

But what is it actually saying?

According to pre-Trib and mid-Trib and even post-Trib theology, how many believers are going to get raptured?

100 percent.

Then why would Jesus tell us to pray for something that is going to happen automatically anyway?

That doesn't make any sense.

If all believers get raptured, why would we have to pray and ask that we could be accounted worthy to escape?

Perhaps if we look at the context of this verse that will give us some clues as to what is actually being said here.

Luke 21 is very, very similar to Matthew 24 and Mark 13. In all three chapters, Jesus describes a period of great tribulation which will unfold before the rapture of the church. And just like in Matthew 24, unusual signs in the sun, the moon and the stars are all mentioned taking place just before the rapture...

25 And there shall be signs in the sun, and in the moon, and in the stars; and upon the earth distress of nations, with perplexity; the sea and the waves roaring;

26 Men's hearts failing them for fear, and for looking after those things which are coming on the earth: for the powers of heaven shall be shaken.

27 And then shall they see the Son of man coming in a cloud with power and great glory.

So Luke 21:36 cannot be talking about a pre-Tribulation rapture, because just like Matthew 24 and Mark 13, Luke 21 puts it at the end of the Tribulation period.

Jesus is not telling us to pray that we might be raptured. If there was going to be a pre-Tribulation rapture, we would all be raptured automatically.

Instead, he is urging us to pray that we "may be accounted worthy to escape all these things that shall come to pass". We aren't going to escape them by being pulled out of the world. Rather, if we are right in the center of God's will there is a good chance that we will be protected even in the midst of all the chaos and the darkness.

This reminds me very much of the words that Jesus prayed in John 17:15...

15 I pray not that thou shouldest take them out of the world, but that thou shouldest keep them from the evil

Once again, the Bible never promises that we will be kept from all tribulation. In fact, the word "tribulation" is used 21 times in the New Testament and none of them have anything to do with the rapture. But many of those verses do promise us that we will face much tribulation as believers. For instance, just consider Acts 14:21-22...

21 And when they had preached the gospel to that city, and had taught many, they returned again to Lystra, and to Iconium, and Antioch,

*22 Confirming the souls of the disciples, and exhorting them to continue in the faith, and **that we must through much tribulation enter into the kingdom of God**.*

If the Bible expressly stated that we were going to be raptured before the Tribulation, that is precisely what would happen.

But the Bible **never** says that.

Instead, those that believe in a pre-Tribulation rapture have to manufacture their theory from verses that they twist and distort.

The idea that God would never want us to go through the Tribulation period because it is going to be too hard is absurd.

What about the believers in ancient Rome that were eaten by lions?

Why didn't they get a rapture?

What about the believers that were put in concentration camps in Nazi Germany, Soviet Russia and Communist China?

Why didn't they get a rapture?

I want to share with you a story that I have shared on my websites that originally comes from The Voice Of The Martyrs (http://www.persecution.com/). This is the kind of suffering that Christians in North Korea have to face...

The young brown-eyed girl looked up at her mother. What would she decide?

Earlier that morning, the young girl's mother, their pastor, and twenty-six others in her North Korean village of GokSan were bound and taken before a screaming crowd of Communists.

One of the guards ordered Pastor Kim and the other Christians, "Deny Christ, or you will die." The words chilled her. How could they ask her to deny Jesus? She knew in her heart he was real. They all quietly refused.

Then the Communist guard shouted directly at the adult Christians, "Deny Christ, or we will hang your children." The young girl looked up at her mother. She gripped her and knowing how much her mom loved her. Her mother then leaned down. With confidence and peace [she] whispered, "Today, my love, I will see you in heaven."

All of the children were hanged.

The remaining believers were then brought out onto the pavement and forced to lie down in front of a large steamroller. The Communists gave them one last chance. "Deny this Jesus or you will be crushed." The Christians had already given up their children; there was no turning back.

As the driver started the heavy piece of equipment, the singing from the villagers started softly. "More love, O Christ, to thee, more love to thee."

This is what believers in North Korea have to deal with, and yet we believe that we are so special that we are automatically going to get a "get out of jail free" card even though the Bible says no such thing.

Well, I have a message for the soft believers of the western world. You better get ready, because we are going to go through the horrors of the Tribulation period, and the greatest wave of persecution that the church has ever experienced is still ahead of us.

-CHAPTER EIGHTEEN-

That Day And Hour

One of the favorite arguments that those that believe in a pre-Tribulation rapture like to use is "nobody will know the day or the hour" of the return of Christ, and therefore the rapture must be a total surprise. Since it must be a total surprise, then it can only come before the Tribulation period.

Sadly, very few people ever challenge pre-Tribbers on this point. One of the places where pre-Tribbers get this is from Matthew 25:13...

13 Watch therefore, ***for ye know neither the day nor the hour*** *wherein the Son of man cometh.*

Another place where they get this from is in Matthew 24...

32 Now learn a parable of the fig tree; When his branch is yet tender, and putteth forth leaves, ye know that summer is nigh:

33 So likewise ye, when ye shall see all these things, know that it is near, even at the doors.

34 Verily I say unto you, This generation shall not pass, till all these things be fulfilled.

35 Heaven and earth shall pass away, but my words shall not pass away.

36 But of that day and hour knoweth no man, no, not the angels of heaven, but my Father only.

When Jesus talks about "the day" or "the hour", what is He referring to?

Both of the passages quoted above are a contin   tion of the
discussion that Jesus was having with His disc   es about the
end times that began at the beginning of Mattl   24. And in
both cases, Jesus is clearly referring to the con   ;
("parousia") that He had just described. It is s   oly not
possible for these verses to refer to a pre-Tribu   ion rapture,
because He had just finished telling His discip   that the
rapture comes "after the tribulation of those da   ". Once
again, let's take a look at what Matthew 24:29-   says...

*29 **Immediately after the tribulation of**   se days*
shall the sun be darkened, and the moon shall   t give her
light, and the stars shall fall from heaven, and   e powers of
the heavens shall be shaken:

30 And then shall appear the sign of the Son o   an in
heaven: and then shall all the tribes of the ear   nourn, and
they shall see the Son of man coming in the clo   's of heaven
with power and great glory.

31 And he shall send his angels with a great so   d of a
trumpet, and they shall gather together his ele   from the
four winds, from one end of heaven to the oth

When Jesus said that no man knows the day o   e hour, this
is the event that he was talking about. It is abs   l for pre-
Tribbers to try to apply Matthew 24:36 or Mat   w 25:13 to a
pre-Tribulation rapture because they don't eve   elieve that
Matthew 24 is talking about the rapture. If the   lid, they
would have to admit that the rapture comes "a   · the
Tribulation of those days".

Secondly, it is very important to keep in mind   t Jesus is
speaking in the present tense in verse 36. We   not take a
statement made in the present tense and turn   ito a
doctrine for all time.

For example, if I told you that it was cloudy outside right now, that would not mean that I was telling you that it would always be cloudy outside forever. Rather, my statement would only apply to the current conditions.

In Mark 13, Jesus goes one step further and tells us that not even He knew the day or the hour at that time. But do you think that He knows now? Yes, I believe that He certainly does. Anyone that believes that He does not runs into some very serious theological problems that go far beyond the timing of the rapture.

It is absolutely crucial to not go beyond what the Word of God actually says. Jesus did not say that nobody would ever know the timing of His return. He simply said that nobody but the Father knew it at that moment in time.

Thirdly, it is so important to know the culture of the day when interpreting Scripture. Rosh Hashanah (also known as Yom Teruah and the Feast of Trumpets) was always called the "day and hour which no man knows" in ancient Israel. The reason for this was the fact that Rosh Hashanah always falls on the first day of the seventh month, and the holiday could not be officially declared until the new moon was spotted. In ancient Israel, the authorities were never quite sure when that would be. The following comes from highly respected Bible scholar Bill Schnoebelen, and you can find it at his website (http://www.withoneaccord.org)...

The rabbis did their best to obscure the prophetic, eschatological meaning of the feast! It has always been called the "day and hour which no man knows." The rabbis try to avoid using that phrase any more. Why was it called that?

Remember, the Father's (Yahuwah's) calendar (not just the Jewish calendar) is LUNAR. That means every Hebrew month begins on the New Moon (Rosh Chodesh in Hebrew – "head of the month"). That is why our calendar is never in sync with the secular Gregorian (Roman) calendar. Yom Teruah (Day of Trumpets) always falls on the New Moon beginning the seventh month (called Tishrei).

The new moons are all prophetic shadow pictures of coming events, but this new moon day of the seventh month is extraordinary, because it begins the fall festivals of Yahuwah.

Yom Teruah was determined according to the Torah by the first sighting of the sliver of the New Moon over Temple Mount. It needed to be sighted by at least two witnesses (Matt. 18:16). When this occurs, the trumpet is blown and the feast officially starts! While any sufficiently advanced society can predict the New Moon with reasonable accuracy, this stipulation throws a Spanner in the works.

If the sliver of the New Moon rises and it's cloudy that evening over Jerusalem, <u>it cannot be seen</u>. Since it cannot be seen, it cannot be "called!" Therefore, no one knows for sure when this feast will take place - no one knows the "day" or "hour" of it's onset.

Are you starting to get the picture?

In Matthew 24, Jesus makes it abundantly clear that the rapture comes "after the tribulation of those days". It is shameful for the pre-Tribbers to pull a verse totally out of context and try to use it as a proof text for a pre-Tribulation rapture.

And in this whole chapter Jesus is trying to make the point that when we see all of these things begin to take place that we should be feverishly getting ready. In verse 32, He even said that "when ye shall see all these things, know that it is near, even at the doors".

We are supposed to know the season of His return, and this should motivate us to get prepared and to be about the work of the Kingdom.

This is the whole point of the parable that Jesus tells at the end of Matthew chapter 24...

45 Who then is a faithful and wise servant, whom his lord hath made ruler over his household, to give them meat in due season?

46 Blessed is that servant, whom his lord when he cometh shall find so doing.

47 Verily I say unto you, That he shall make him ruler over all his goods.

48 But and if that evil servant shall say in his heart, My lord delayeth his coming;

49 And shall begin to smite his fellowservants, and to eat and drink with the drunken;

50 The lord of that servant shall come in a day when he looketh not for him, and in an hour that he is not aware of,

51 And shall cut him asunder, and appoint him his portion with the hypocrites: there shall be weeping and gnashing of teeth.

There is so much work to be done. Whatever amount of time we have left before the return of Jesus, that is all the time we have remaining to bring in the rest of the harvest.

Sadly, millions of believers are not even planning to participate in the great harvest that is coming because they have already checked out on life because they believe that a pre-Tribulation rapture is imminent.

That is incredibly sad, because I believe that the greatest move of God the world has ever seen is coming. Everything that can be shaken will be shaken, and all of this shaking is going to result in an unprecedented harvest for the Kingdom of God. This is something that I will discuss much more in a future chapter. But for now, let's continue dismantling some of the favorite arguments that pre-Tribbers like to use...

-CHAPTER NINETEEN-

A Thief In The Night?

In 1972, a Christian filmmaker named Russell S. Doughten released a movie entitled "A Thief In The Night" which featured a pre-Tribulation rapture, and it took the Christian world by storm. It has been estimated that this one film was seen by at least 300 million people around the world, and it spawned three sequels: "A Distant Thunder" (1978), "Image Of The Beast" (1981) and "The Prodigal Planet" (1983).

When I was a young boy, the church that my family was attending played this film for us, and it had a very deep impact on me. I was deathly afraid of a world where everyone was being forced to take the Mark of the Beast, and so I was very happy that a pre-Tribulation rapture was coming to keep us all from going through that. Of course at that time there was nobody to tell me the other side of the story. In those days it seemed like virtually everyone in the evangelical Christian world believed in a pre-Tribulation rapture.

Following the release of that movie, the saying that Jesus is coming "as a thief in the night" became very popular among Christians. In fact, this one phrase was often used to immediately shut down any arguments against a pre-Tribulation rapture. After all, that is exactly what the Bible says, right?

The following is what the first three verses of 1 Thessalonians chapter 5 say...

But of the times and the seasons, brethren, ye have no need that I write unto you.

*2 For yourselves know perfectly that the day of the Lord so cometh **as a thief in the night.***

3 For when they shall say, Peace and safety; then sudden destruction cometh upon them, as travail upon a woman with child; and they shall not escape.

Earlier in this book we already covered the fact that it is "the day of the Lord" and not the Tribulation that comes as a thief in the night.

Now, I want to continue looking at the rest of this passage in 1 Thessalonians 5. Many of those that believe in a pre-Tribulation rapture continue to quote verse 2 as a "proof text" for a pre-Tribulation rapture to this very day. If only they would read the verses that immediately follow...

*4 **But ye, brethren, are not in darkness, that that day should overtake you as a thief**.*

5 Ye are all the children of light, and the children of the day: we are not of the night, nor of darkness.

Just two verses after we are told that the Lord is coming "as a thief in the night", we are told that we are not in darkness and therefore His coming **should not overtake us as a thief**.

The rapture is not supposed to be a surprise for those of us that are believers. There is so much confusion in the body of Christ today about the timing of the rapture, but the Scriptures are actually exceedingly clear. In the next letter that he sent to the Thessalonians, the Apostle Paul told them that there are certain signs to watch for that must happen before the rapture takes place. I know that I have discussed the first portion of 2 Thessalonians chapter 2 already in this book, but it bears repeating. This passage alone completely rules out a pre-Tribulation rapture...

Now we beseech you, brethren, by the **coming** *("**parousia**") of our Lord Jesus Christ, and by* **our gathering together unto him,**

2 That ye be not soon shaken in mind, or be troubled, neither by spirit, nor by word, nor by letter as from us, as that the day of Christ is at hand.

3 **Let no man deceive you by any means: for that day shall not come, except there come a falling away first, and that man of sin be revealed, the son of perdition;**

4 **Who opposeth and exalteth himself above all that is called God, or that is worshipped; so that he as God sitteth in the temple of God, shewing himself that he is God.**

5 Remember ye not, that, when I was yet with you, I told you these things?

The Bible is very clear – there are certain things that must take place before the rapture, and one of them is the defiling of a rebuilt Jewish temple in Jerusalem by the Antichrist. This event was first prophesied in Daniel chapter 9...

27 And he shall confirm the covenant with many for one week: and in the midst of the week he shall cause the sacrifice and the oblation to cease, and for the overspreading of abominations he shall make it desolate, even until the consummation, and that determined shall be poured upon the desolate.

This verse talks about a period of time that has come to be known as "Daniel's 70th week", and it indicates that the Antichrist will defile the temple in the middle of the seven year Tribulation period.

In Matthew 24, Jesus refers to the writings of the prophet Daniel, and He tells us that this "abomination of desolation" will set off the greatest period of persecution that believers have ever known...

15 When ye therefore shall see the abomination of desolation, spoken of by Daniel the prophet, stand in the holy place, (whoso readeth, let him understand:)

16 Then let them which be in Judaea flee into the mountains:

17 Let him which is on the housetop not come down to take any thing out of his house:

18 Neither let him which is in the field return back to take his clothes.

19 And woe unto them that are with child, and to them that give suck in those days!

20 But pray ye that your flight be not in the winter, neither on the sabbath day:

21 For then shall be great tribulation, such as was not since the beginning of the world to this time, no, nor ever shall be.

Just like the Apostle Paul, the Lord Jesus is very clear about the fact that the abomination of desolation comes before the rapture. Following the abomination of desolation, there will be a three and a half year period during which the Antichrist conducts a vicious war against the saints, and then the rapture will finally come. Later on in Matthew 24 we find the following description of the rapture...

29 **Immediately after the tribulation of those days** *shall the sun be darkened, and the moon shall not give her light, and the stars shall fall from heaven, and the powers of the heavens shall be shaken:*

30 And then shall appear the sign of the Son of man in heaven: and then shall all the tribes of the earth mourn, and they shall see the Son of man coming in the clouds of heaven with power and great glory.

31 **And he shall send his angels with a great sound of a trumpet, and they shall gather together his elect from the four winds, from one end of heaven to the other***.*

I know that I am repeating some of these passages quite a few times in this book, but it is absolutely imperative that you see how all of these pieces interrelate.

And if "a thief in the night" refers to a pre-Tribulation rapture, then why does the Lord Jesus say "I come as a thief" in Revelation chapter 16 just before the Battle of Armageddon at the end of the Tribulation period?...

15 Behold, **I come as a thief***. Blessed is he that watcheth, and keepeth his garments, lest he walk naked, and they see his shame.*

God is not trying to trick us. The truth is that all of these passages are very consistent and they contain the exact same message. The rapture comes **after** the Tribulation and not before.

But because most evangelical churches in America are teaching a pre-Tribulation rapture, most Christians are not getting ready for what is ahead.

When it was released in 1972, "A Thief In The Night" featured a wonderful song by Larry Norman entitled "I Wish We'd All Been Ready" that went on to become one of the most popular Christian anthems of the 1970s. It was written from a pre-Tribulation rapture perspective, but I think that some of the lyrics could definitely apply to millions of Christians today that are not getting prepared for the future because of their mistaken belief that a pre-Tribulation rapture is going to whisk them away before anything really bad can happen...

Life was filled with guns and war

And all of us got trampled on the floor

I wish we'd all been ready

The children died, the days grew cold

A piece of bread could buy a bag of gold

I wish we'd all been ready

What about you?

Are you getting ready mentally, emotionally, financially, physically and spiritually for the very difficult years that are ahead?

I certainly hope so, because they will be upon us sooner than most people would dare to imagine.

-CHAPTER TWENTY-

The Restrainer

In the last chapter we looked at the first five verses of 2 Thessalonians 2, and in this chapter we will look at the next five verses. One of the all-time favorite arguments that those that believe in a pre-Tribulation rapture like to use is the one about "the restrainer" described in 2 Thessalonians 2:6-7. Typically, the argument goes something like this - since the Holy Spirit is the "restrainer", and the Holy Spirit lives in all believers, then all believers must be raptured off the planet before the Antichrist can be revealed. This is what 2 Thessalonians 2:6-10 says in the King James version...

6 And now ye know what withholdeth that he might be revealed in his time.

7 For the mystery of iniquity doth already work: only he who now letteth will let, until he be taken out of the way.

8 And then shall that Wicked be revealed, whom the Lord shall consume with the spirit of his mouth, and shall destroy with the brightness of his coming:

9 Even him, whose coming is after the working of Satan with all power and signs and lying wonders,

10 And with all deceivableness of unrighteousness in them that perish; because they received not the love of the truth, that they might be saved.

Where pre-Trib advocates get the term "restrainer" is from later English translations of the Bible such as the New American Standard version...

6 And you know what restrains him now, so that in his time he will be revealed.

7 For the mystery of lawlessness is already at work; only he who now restrains will do so until he is taken out of the way.

On a very basic level, this argument would seem to make some sense. The verses above could certainly be interpreted to mean that something is holding the Antichrist back from being revealed right now, and certainly the Holy Spirit would be powerful enough to do that.

There is just one absolutely massive problem. The first five verses of 2 Thessalonians 2 already made it abundantly clear that the rapture will not happen until **after** the Antichrist is revealed. If you did not catch this from the last chapter, go back and read it again.

The way that pre-Trib advocates interpret this passage has the Apostle Paul directly contradicting himself **in the exact same chapter**. It makes absolutely no sense for the Apostle Paul to say that the rapture will take place after the Antichrist is revealed in verses one through four, only later to completely reverse that order in verses six and seven.

Let's use a little common sense here.

And if the presence of the Holy Spirit in Christians is able to "restrain" the Antichrist, then why couldn't we do anything to restrain much lesser tyrants throughout history?

Why couldn't we "restrain" Hitler?

Why couldn't we "restrain" Stalin?

Why couldn't we "restrain" Mao?

Here in the United States, the church couldn't even keep Barack Obama from getting elected.

And yet we are going to "restrain" the Antichrist?

In addition, those that claim that the Holy Spirit will no longer be present on our planet after a pre-Tribulation rapture are presented with some massive challenges by the book of Revelation.

For example, in Revelation 11 we are told that the two witnesses are able to prophesy, do miracles and hit the earth with plagues...

3 And I will give power unto my two witnesses, and they shall prophesy a thousand two hundred and threescore days, clothed in sackcloth.

4 These are the two olive trees, and the two candlesticks standing before the God of the earth.

5 And if any man will hurt them, fire proceedeth out of their mouth, and devoureth their enemies: and if any man will hurt them, he must in this manner be killed.

6 These have power to shut heaven, that it rain not in the days of their prophecy: and have power over waters to turn them to blood, and to smite the earth with all plagues, as often as they will.

Are these two witnesses doing these things without the power of the Holy Spirit?

If so, where are they getting the power?

In Revelation 12, we read about how believers during the Tribulation are able to overcome the enemy "by the blood of the Lamb, and by the word of their testimony". Once again, are we supposed to believe that they are doing this without the Holy Spirit's help at all?

Theologians have been debating who "the restrainer" is for centuries, and they will continue to debate this until Jesus comes back. It is one of those things in Scripture that is not exceedingly clear, and that is okay.

Even if it is the Holy Spirit that is restraining the Antichrist, that does not mean that He has to completely be removed from this planet for the restraining to stop. I think that a very simple illustration would be helpful here. If I am holding one of my cats and "restraining" her from chasing a mouse that is running across the other side of the room, I don't have to completely remove myself from the house to release her. No, all I have to do is open up my hands and she will be free to jump away and race after the little rodent.

Similarly, the Holy Spirit does not have to leave the entire planet in order for the Antichrist to no longer be restrained. He could most certainly allow the lawless one to come forth and remain active in our world at the same time. Anyone that argues otherwise is just not using common sense.

Those that argue that 2 Thessalonians 2:6-7 is clear evidence for a pre-Tribulation rapture are being more than just a little bit disingenuous. Yes, I know that they are reaching for straws, but they would do better to avoid a chapter that very clearly teaches that the Antichrist will be revealed **before** the rapture.

As for the true identity of the restrainer, there is a theological principle that the unclear is to be interpreted in light of the clear.

Some believe that the restrainer is the Holy Spirit, others believe that it is the archangel Michael, and others believe that this passage is actually saying that the forces of darkness are the ones doing the "restraining". I have listened to a multitude of teachings about this personally, and I consider it to be one of those things that is definitely open for debate.

But no matter what side of the debate you come down on, no interpretation of this passage can contradict the very clear teaching in the first five verses of 2 Thessalonians 2 that the rapture comes **after** the revealing of the Antichrist. Anyone that tells you any differently is not being honest with you.

-CHAPTER TWENTY ONE-

The Blessed Hope

In recent years, "the blessed hope" has become synonymous with a pre-Tribulation rapture in evangelical Christian circles. In fact, the phrase is used so frequently in connection with a pre-Tribulation rapture that you know exactly what someone is referring to the moment that it is used.

But where does this phrase actually come from?

It comes from Titus chapter 2...

11 For the grace of God that bringeth salvation hath appeared to all men,

12 Teaching us that, denying ungodliness and worldly lusts, we should live soberly, righteously, and godly, in this present world;

*13 **Looking for that blessed hope, and the glorious appearing of the great God and our Saviour Jesus Christ;***

14 Who gave himself for us, that he might redeem us from all iniquity, and purify unto himself a peculiar people, zealous of good works.

As you can see, there is absolutely nothing to indicate that the rapture will occur before the Tribulation in that passage. And yet pre-Trib advocates continue to use this phrase as if there is rock solid evidence that it refers to a pre-Tribulation rapture.

All believers are looking forward to the return of our Lord and Savior Jesus Christ. So we are all eagerly anticipating "the blessed hope". But if you start to bring up the passages that clearly indicate that the rapture will not happen before the Tribulation, some pre-Trib advocates will actually accuse you of "stealing the blessed hope" from people. I have actually seen video footage of a Christian conference where this happened. And if you can believe it, there are some pre-Trib advocates that are now running around accusing anyone that does not believe in a pre-Tribulation rapture of being a "heretic" and of purposely trying to get people to look for the appearance of the Antichrist instead of looking for the appearance of Christ.

Of course the truth is that God gave us very specific signs to watch for before the return of Jesus **so that we would not be deceived**. I know that I have used 2 Thessalonians 2 several times already, but let us go over it one more time. The Bible very clearly teaches that the Antichrist will be revealed **before** the rapture takes place...

*Now we beseech you, brethren, by the coming of our Lord Jesus Christ, and by **our gathering together unto him**,*

2 That ye be not soon shaken in mind, or be troubled, neither by spirit, nor by word, nor by letter as from us, as that the day of Christ is at hand.

3 Let no man deceive you by any means: for that day shall not come, except there come a falling away first, and that man of sin be revealed, the son of perdition;

4 Who opposeth and exalteth himself above all that is called God, or that is worshipped; so that he as God sitteth in the temple of God, shewing himself that he is God.

So how are we hurting people by telling them the truth?

The Antichrist comes before Jesus does.

There should be no debate.

God warns us about these things so that we can be prepared ahead of time.

But those preaching a pre-Tribulation rapture are not preparing the bride for the persecution to come. Instead, they are equating "the blessed hope" with escape from persecution.

Somehow, they are arrogant enough to believe that the lukewarm, half-hearted Christians of the 21st century are so special that they are going to get to avoid the kinds of trials and tribulations that believers all throughout history have had to endure.

Hebrews 11 is known as "the Hall of Faith", and toward the end of the chapter it describes what many of the men and women of God before the time of Christ suffered for their faith...

*35 Women received their dead raised to life again: and others were **tortured**, not accepting deliverance; that they might obtain a better resurrection:*

*36 And others had trial of **cruel mockings** and **scourgings**, yea, moreover of **bonds** and **imprisonment**:*

*37 They were **stoned**, they were **sawn asunder**, were tempted, were **slain with the sword**: they wandered about in sheepskins and goatskins; being **destitute**, **afflicted**, **tormented**;*

38 (Of whom the world was not worthy:) **they wandered in deserts, and in mountains, and in dens and caves of the earth.**

Could you imagine being cut in two with a saw?

Of course virtually all of the apostles were killed for their faith. Some early Christian leaders were stoned, others were killed by sword or spear, and some were even reportedly crucified upside down.

Later on, the Roman Empire invented even more sadistic ways to kill Christians. Entire families were fed to lions, and one emperor even lit the roads with the burning bodies of Christians that he had killed.

During the Dark Ages, the popes of Roman Catholicism tortured and killed millions upon millions of believers that did not submit to their authority. Great men of God were burned at the stake for "crimes" such as translating the Bible into English and preaching a gospel of salvation by faith.

Even today, Christians are being raped, tortured, beheaded and crucified by radical Islamic groups in the Middle East such as ISIS.

But evangelical Christians in America are so special and so holy that we get a free pass?

I don't think so.

In fact, this is what my Bible says in 2 Timothy 3:12…

*Yea, and **all** that will live godly in Christ Jesus **shall suffer persecution**.*

And of course there are lots more passages just like this all throughout the New Testament. For instance, just consider 1

Thessalonians 3:2-4. In this case, I have used the Modern English Version (MEV)...

2 We sent Timothy, who is our brother and minister of God and our fellow laborer in the gospel of Christ, to establish and comfort you with regard to your faith,

3 so that no one would be shaken by these afflictions. **For you know that we are appointed to this.**

4 Indeed, we told you before when we were with you **that we would suffer tribulation,** *just as it came to pass, as you well know.*

If the Bible actually did teach a pre-Tribulation rapture, that would be one thing.

But it doesn't.

Instead, those that teach a pre-Tribulation rapture are engaged in the same kind of wishful thinking that those that teach the "prosperity gospel" are engaging in.

Telling people what they want to hear may promote church attendance and it may bring in larger offerings, but it is an exceedingly cruel thing to do.

There are thousands of pastors out there that should be preparing the bride of Christ for what is about to happen, but instead they are taking the easy road. Since most American Christians have embraced it anyway, it is really easy to preach a pre-Tribulation rapture.

But what is going to happen when the Tribulation comes and there is no rapture?

Millions upon millions of Christians will be faced with horrors that they have never been prepared for. Many will deeply question their faith, countless numbers will give in to despair and depression, and some may even commit suicide so that they can get the "escape" that they were promised.

But God does not want us to be fearful of what is coming. He knows everything that is going to happen in advance, He is in control, and He has a plan for each one of us and our families.

Personally, my wife and I strive to live in a constant state of "shalom", which is the Hebrew word for peace. We believe that the greatest chapters of our lives will be in the midst of all the chaos and darkness that is coming. We are greatly looking forward to what is ahead, because we believe that the greatest move of God and the greatest harvest of souls the world has ever seen are rapidly approaching. I will go into all of this much more in future chapters.

Sadly, most Christians are not getting prepared for the hard times that are ahead of us, and they don't want to hear about the amazing things that God is about to do because they believe that they are about to get pulled out of here.

They are kind of like people at a wonderful party that are hanging out by the door the whole time because they expect their rides to show up at any moment.

In the end, millions of Christians in America are going to die waiting for a pre-Tribulation rapture that is never going to happen.

This could have been avoided if Christian leaders had been willing to tell the truth, but that didn't happen, and now the consequences will be almost too horrible for words.

-CHAPTER TWENTY TWO-

Come Up Hither

Today, if you ask many pre-Trib advocates to show you where the rapture is located in the book of Revelation, they will take you directly to Revelation chapter 4. In their desperation to put the rapture "where it should be" in the book of Revelation, those that believe in a pre-Tribulation rapture have increasingly become willing to read things into certain passages which simply are not there.

As Revelation chapter 4 begins, Jesus had just given the Apostle John seven letters for seven churches, and now John is being called up to heaven to appear before the throne of God. The following are the first two verses of Revelation 4 in the MEV. Read carefully and see if you can spot where the rapture is clearly described...

After this I looked. And there was an open door in heaven. The first voice I heard was like a trumpet speaking with me, saying, "Come up here, and I will show you things which must take place after this." 2 Immediately I was in the Spirit. And there was a throne set in heaven with One sitting on the throne!

Did you see it?

Go back and read it again if you missed it.

You still can't find it?

Well, the reason you can't find it is because it isn't in there.

The technical theological term for what pre-Trib advocates are doing is "making stuff up".

Actually, I am kidding. There is a technical term for what they are doing and it is called "eisegesis". Wikipedia defines eisegesis as "the process of interpreting a text or portion of text in such a way that the process introduces one's own presuppositions, agendas, or biases into and onto the text."

Let me try to summarize the argument that those that believe in a pre-Tribulation rapture are attempting to make. The first three chapters of the book of Revelation contain seven letters to seven churches. Many believe that these seven letters correspond to seven specific periods of time within the "church age", and the phrase "things which must be hereafter" in Revelation 4:1 is referring to events which come immediately after the church age.

So it makes perfect sense to them that when the Apostle John is told to "come up hither" in the first verse of Revelation 4, that it is code for the rapture. Since Revelation 4 immediately follows the church age described in the first three chapters, a pre-Tribulation rapture would fit very, very nicely right there.

Pre-Trib advocates also like to point out that the word "church" is never used after Revelation 4. And this is true, but numerous references are made to believers living on the earth all throughout the book of Revelation (Revelation 7:3-8; 11:3-6; 12:11; 12:17; 13:7-10; 14:12). How those that believe in a pre-Tribulation rapture get around this is by labeling those believers as "Tribulation saints". The idea is that once the pre-Tribulation rapture occurs, millions of people that realize that they have been "left behind" will regret their mistake and will quickly give their lives to the Lord. Somehow this will happen without any help from the Holy Spirit, because since He is "the restrainer", He will be completely removed from the earth at the time of the rapture. This is something that I covered in a previous chapter.

As you can see, it all gets very complicated. If you want to believe in a pre-Tribulation rapture, you have to jump through all sorts of mental hoops. But since it is taught in most evangelical churches in America today, most Christians typically don't question the mental gymnastics.

The only way that you can believe that the rapture is in Revelation chapter 4 is if you have an exceedingly active imagination.

And if you want to try to put the rapture in Revelation chapter 4, that would directly contradict the rest of the book of Revelation. As we have already seen in this book, the rapture is announced in Revelation 11, and it is very clearly described in Revelation 14...

14 And I looked, and behold a white cloud, and upon the cloud one sat like unto the Son of man, having on his head a golden crown, and in his hand a sharp sickle.

15 And another angel came out of the temple, crying with a loud voice to him that sat on the cloud, Thrust in thy sickle, and reap: for the time is come for thee to reap; for the harvest of the earth is ripe.

16 And he that sat on the cloud thrust in his sickle on the earth; and the earth was reaped.

If you will remember, this comes after the seventh trumpet (the last trumpet) is blown, but before any of the vial judgments are poured out. In this passage we see the Son of Man with a crown upon his head standing upon a white cloud. He harvests the earth, and subsequently the full measure of God's wrath is poured out on those that remain on this planet.

From Revelation 14:14 on, there are no more mentions of believers on this planet until we return with Jesus in Revelation 19. But in Revelation 15 we do see a scene in heaven that includes believers that have gotten the victory over the Antichrist...

2 And I saw as it were a sea of glass mingled with fire: **and them that had gotten the victory over the beast, and over his image, and over his mark, and over the number of his name,** *stand on the sea of glass, having the harps of God.*

3 And they sing the song of Moses the servant of God, and the song of the Lamb, saying, Great and marvellous are thy works, Lord God Almighty; just and true are thy ways, thou King of saints.

4 Who shall not fear thee, O Lord, and glorify thy name? for thou only art holy: for all nations shall come and worship before thee; for thy judgments are made manifest.

So how did those "Tribulation saints" get there if the rapture took place all the way back in Revelation 4?

And how do those that believe in a pre-Tribulation rapture account for the rapture described in Revelation 14:14-16?

Actually, theories that contain "multiple raptures" have become increasingly popular in pre-Trib circles in recent years. But most pre-Trib advocates attempt to get around the rapture of Revelation 14 by ignoring it altogether.

In addition, how can the rapture be in chapter 4 when Revelation chapter 20 says that "the first resurrection" comes at the very end of the Tribulation?

Hopefully this book will help ordinary believers to see that we should not be trying to force the Bible to fit into our particular pet theories about the end times.

Instead, we should just be willing to believe the plain meaning of the text. And what the Scriptures tell us is very clear – the rapture comes at the end of the Tribulation period and not at the beginning.

-CHAPTER TWENTY THREE-

The Best Evidence For A Pre-Tribulation Rapture

In this chapter, I am going to share with you the very best evidence for a pre-Tribulation rapture.

Yes, I am being completely serious.

I believed in a pre-Tribulation rapture most of my life, and I have studied the works of some of the greatest pre-Trib scholars of all time. I am familiar with all of the arguments, and we have already gone over many of them.

But there is one passage that we haven't looked at yet, and to me it is the strongest argument that pre-Trib advocates have by a long shot. If I was trying to convince people that a pre-Tribulation rapture was going to happen, this is the very first place that I would go.

This is what Revelation chapter 7 says starting in verse 9...

9 After this I beheld, and, lo, a great multitude, which no man could number, of all nations, and kindreds, and people, and tongues, stood before the throne, and before the Lamb, clothed with white robes, and palms in their hands;

10 And cried with a loud voice, saying, Salvation to our God which sitteth upon the throne, and unto the Lamb.

11 And all the angels stood round about the throne, and about the elders and the four beasts, and fell before the throne on their faces, and worshipped God,

12 Saying, Amen: Blessing, and glory, and wisdom, and thanksgiving, and honour, and power, and might, be unto our God for ever and ever. Amen.

13 And one of the elders answered, saying unto me, What are these which are arrayed in white robes? and whence came they?

*14 And I said unto him, Sir, thou knowest. And he said to me, **These are they which came out of great tribulation**, and have washed their robes, and made them white in the blood of the Lamb.*

15 Therefore are they before the throne of God, and serve him day and night in his temple: and he that sitteth on the throne shall dwell among them.

16 They shall hunger no more, neither thirst any more; neither shall the sun light on them, nor any heat.

17 For the Lamb which is in the midst of the throne shall feed them, and shall lead them unto living fountains of waters: and God shall wipe away all tears from their eyes.

In this passage we clearly see a very large gathering of believers in heaven singing praises to God. When the Apostle John asks about this group of believers, he is told that they "came out of the great tribulation".

At first glance, this passage certainly sounds very promising for a pre-Tribulation rapture position. But actually, upon further examination it seems to fit much better with a mid-Trib point of view.

John is told that this group of believers "came out of the great tribulation", which seems to imply that the Tribulation is already taking place. For example, you don't talk about a player "coming out of the game" if he left the ballpark before the game even began. So without a doubt, that phrase is a problem for pre-Trib advocates.

Another problem for pre-Tribbers is the fact that we don't read about this gathering until after the first six seals have been opened. So those that believe in a pre-Trib rapture have to argue that either the six seals take place before the Tribulation period begins or that the gathering in Revelation 7 is of believers that were raptured at some earlier time. Mid-Trib advocates don't have the same problem, because many of them believe that the rapture takes place near the end of the seal judgments.

Lastly, earlier in chapter 7 we read about 144,000 "servants of God" that are still on the earth being sealed. So why are they still on the earth while this other vast multitude is in heaven? Somehow pre-Tribbers and mid-Tribbers have to argue that the 144,000 were miraculously saved just after the rapture took place.

But without a doubt, this passage does pose some issues for those that believe in a post-Tribulation rapture. Primarily, we have to deal with the fact that there is this vast multitude of believers standing in heaven before the throne of God before the end of the Tribulation period.

So how did they get there?

Well, there are just two options. Either they **died** or they were **raptured**.

There is absolutely no mention of a resurrection or resurrected bodies in Revelation 7 or in the surrounding context, and that is something that we would hope to see in the text if indeed a rapture had just taken place.

I would submit that the more likely explanation is that what is happening here is that this is a group of Christians that has died and gone to heaven. Remember, Revelation 7 immediately follows the horrifying seal judgments of Revelation 6. In Revelation 6:8 we read that a "fourth part of the earth" is killed "with sword, and with hunger, and with death, and with the beasts of the earth" when the fourth seal is opened. And the opening of the sixth seal sounds like one of the greatest natural disasters in human history...

12 And I beheld when he had opened the sixth seal, and, lo, there was a great earthquake; and the sun became black as sackcloth of hair, and the moon became as blood;

13 And the stars of heaven fell unto the earth, even as a fig tree casteth her untimely figs, when she is shaken of a mighty wind.

14 And the heaven departed as a scroll when it is rolled together; and every mountain and island were moved out of their places.

15 And the kings of the earth, and the great men, and the rich men, and the chief captains, and the mighty men, and every bondman, and every free man, hid themselves in the dens and in the rocks of the mountains;

16 And said to the mountains and rocks, Fall on us, and hide us from the face of him that sitteth on the throne, and from the wrath of the Lamb:

17 For the great day of his wrath is come; and who shall be able to stand?

In addition, let's remember that at the opening of the fifth seal we are introduced to a group of believers "that were slain for the word of God, and for the testimony which they held"...

9 And when he had opened the fifth seal, I saw under the altar the souls of them that were slain for the word of God, and for the testimony which they held:

10 And they cried with a loud voice, saying, How long, O Lord, holy and true, dost thou not judge and avenge our blood on them that dwell on the earth?

11 And white robes were given unto every one of them; and it was said unto them, that they should rest yet for a little season, until their fellowservants also and their brethren, that should be killed as they were, should be fulfilled.

So the Bible clearly tells us that by the opening of the fifth seal a significant number of Christians will have been killed for what they believe, and that more of their brothers and sisters will be "killed as they were" afterwards. Would the time between the opening of the fifth seal and the opening of the sixth seal really be enough time for that?

I don't think so.

Overall, during the seal judgments hundreds of millions of people will die at a minimum. By the time it is all said and done, the death toll could be in the billions.

Without a doubt, many of the dead will be Christians. And I believe that those dead believers are those "which came out of the great tribulation" in Revelation 7.

In order to come to a different conclusion, you have to argue that Revelation 7 directly contradicts Matthew 24, Mark 13, Luke 21, 2 Thessalonians 2 and all of the other scriptures which clearly teach that the rapture takes place after the Tribulation period.

You also have to argue that Revelation 7 directly contradicts what Revelation 11, Revelation 14 and Revelation 20 have to say about the rapture coming at the end of the Tribulation period.

You can try to argue all of that if you want, but then you can't also claim that you believe in the inerrancy of the Word of God.

If Revelation 7 clearly stated that the rapture came before or in the middle of the Tribulation, then that is what we should all believe.

But it doesn't. Instead, in Revelation 7 we see one group of believers that is still on earth being "sealed", and another group of believers in heaven singing praises to God.

The simplest explanation, and the explanation that is the most consistent with the rest of the Bible, is that the believers that we see in heaven in Revelation 7 are those that died during the seal judgments.

-CHAPTER TWENTY FOUR-

The Best Evidence For A Mid-Tribulation Rapture

In recent years, the concept of a mid-Tribulation rapture has become increasingly popular in the United States. It is still very much a minority position, but the ranks of the mid-Tribbers are growing. I think that a lot of people are waking up to the fact that the Bible tells us that there is not going to be a pre-Tribulation rapture, but there is still a lot of confusion about where the rapture actually falls in the book of Revelation. In this book, I have attempted to clear a lot of that confusion up.

For those that take a mid-Trib or a pre-Wrath position, much of the focus is on the passages in the Bible that tell us that we are "not appointed to wrath". This is something that I have dealt with in chapter sixteen and elsewhere in this book, so I am not going to repeat those arguments here. Clearly, the Bible does not promise us that we are not going to have to go through any hard times. In fact, the Scriptures tell us just the opposite.

If I was going to try to convince someone that there was going to be a mid-Trib or a pre-Wrath rapture, I would focus on something else instead. If you look at the events that happen at the sixth seal in Revelation chapter 6 and compare them to the things that Jesus said will take place immediately prior to His return, there appear to be some striking parallels at first glance. Let me show you the two passages I am talking about and you can see for yourself. First, here is Revelation 6:12-17...

12 And I beheld when he had opened the sixth seal, and, lo, there was a great earthquake; and the sun became black as sackcloth of hair, and the moon became as blood;

13 And the stars of heaven fell unto the earth, even as a fig tree casteth her untimely figs, when she is shaken of a mighty wind.

14 And the heaven departed as a scroll when it is rolled together; and every mountain and island were moved out of their places.

15 And the kings of the earth, and the great men, and the rich men, and the chief captains, and the mighty men, and every bondman, and every free man, hid themselves in the dens and in the rocks of the mountains;

16 And said to the mountains and rocks, Fall on us, and hide us from the face of him that sitteth on the throne, and from the wrath of the Lamb:

17 For the great day of his wrath is come; and who shall be able to stand?

With those verses in mind, now consider what Jesus tells us in Matthew 24:29-31...

29 Immediately after the tribulation of those days shall the sun be darkened, and the moon shall not give her light, and the stars shall fall from heaven, and the powers of the heavens shall be shaken:

30 And then shall appear the sign of the Son of man in heaven: and then shall all the tribes of the earth mourn, and they shall see the Son of man coming in the clouds of heaven with power and great glory.

31 And he shall send his angels with a great sound of a trumpet, and they shall gather together his elect from the four winds, from one end of heaven to the other.

So do we have a direct match?

Many of those that advocate a mid-Trib position insist that we do, and therefore they believe that the rapture described in Matthew 24 must happen at the exact same time as the sixth seal.

Of course this would contradict **dozens** of passages that we have already looked at in this book that tell us that the rapture comes immediately **after** the Tribulation. But you have to admit that the similarity between Matthew 24 and Revelation 6 is rather striking – at least at first glance.

Some post-Tribbers get around this by trying to claim that the book of Revelation is not written in chronological order. In particular, they claim that the seals, trumpets and vials all "overlap", and that the sixth seal comes right at the end of the Tribulation period.

Personally, I do not find that argument persuasive at all. You run into all sorts of logical errors once you take a non-chronological view of the seals, trumpets and vials. For instance, the seal judgments do not even mention the Antichrist, and yet the very first vial judgment is poured on out on those that have the Mark of the Beast. I could go on and on, but I do not think that is necessary. In my view, the book of Revelation makes it exceedingly clear that the seals, trumpets and vials take place in chronological order.

So then what are we to make of the parallels between Matthew 24 and Revelation 6?

Well, let's take a closer look at the two passages. As I have noted elsewhere in this book, sometimes looking at the Greek can tell us things that we would not see while reading an English translation of the Bible. And that is definitely true in this case.

Let's start with what happens to the sun. In Matthew 24 we are told that the sun will be "darkened". In the Greek, the word "skotizo" is used, and it means "to cover with darkness" or "to darken".

But in Revelation 6, the Greek word "skotizo" is not found. Instead, an entirely different Greek word is employed. There, the Greek word "melas" is used, and it means "black" or "black ink". From the surrounding context, we get the impression that this is a temporary blacking out of the sun, and indeed the sun is apparently working normally as we proceed along further in the book of Revelation.

And of course this is not the only time that the sun is darkened in the book of Revelation. The sun is "smitten" when the fourth angel sounds his trumpet in Revelation chapter 8, the sun is "darkened" when the bottomless pit is opened in Revelation chapter 9, and the kingdom of Antichrist is plunged into darkness when the fifth angel pours out his vial in Revelation 16.

So when it comes to the darkening of the sun, there are certainly a lot of potential matches.

Next, let's take a look at what happens to the moon. In Matthew 24, we are told that the moon "shall not give her light", but in Revelation 6 we are told that the moon "became as blood". **In order for the moon to be blood red in appearance, light must be coming from the moon.** This is basic science. So instead of being a "match", Matthew 24 and Revelation 6 seem to be saying two contradictory things. In Matthew 24, the moon is not giving off any light at all, but in Revelation 6 the moon is giving off red light.

If that is the case, how can those two passages be describing the same event?

Matthew 24 is definitely talking about the rapture, and if Revelation chapter 6 was talking about the same moment in time, we would expect to see at least some mention of the rapture there as well.

But we don't.

Instead, we find the rapture announced much later when the seventh trumpet is blown in Revelation 11, and then we find a very clear description of the rapture event itself in Revelation chapter 14 before the vial judgments are poured out. The rapture is in the book of Revelation exactly where the rest of the Bible says it should be, and this is something that I covered earlier in this book.

So in my humble opinion, we do not have a "match" between Matthew 24 and Revelation 6.

But we do have a perfect "match" between Matthew 24 and two other key passages.

One of them is Joel chapter 2. In fact, you may have a Bible that has a footnote in Matthew 24 that points you directly to Joel 2:10. Here is Joel 2:10 in context...

Blow ye the trumpet in Zion, and sound an alarm in my holy mountain: let all the inhabitants of the land tremble: ***for the day of the Lord cometh,*** *for it is nigh at hand;*

2 A day of darkness and of gloominess, a day of clouds and of thick darkness, as the morning spread upon the mountains: a great people and a strong; there hath not been ever the like, neither shall be any more after it, even to the years of many generations.

3 A fire devoureth before them; and behind them a flame burneth: the land is as the garden of Eden before them, and behind them a desolate wilderness; yea, and nothing shall escape them.

4 The appearance of them is as the appearance of horses; and as horsemen, so shall they run.

5 Like the noise of chariots on the tops of mountains shall they leap, like the noise of a flame of fire that devoureth the stubble, as a strong people set in battle array.

6 Before their face the people shall be much pained: all faces shall gather blackness.

7 They shall run like mighty men; they shall climb the wall like men of war; and they shall march every one on his ways, and they shall not break their ranks:

8 Neither shall one thrust another; they shall walk every one in his path: and when they fall upon the sword, they shall not be wounded.

9 They shall run to and fro in the city; they shall run upon the wall, they shall climb up upon the houses; they shall enter in at the windows like a thief.

10 The earth shall quake before them; the heavens shall tremble: the sun and the moon shall be dark, and the stars shall withdraw their shining:

11 And the Lord shall utter his voice before his army: for his camp is very great: for he is strong that executeth his word: for the day of the Lord is great and very terrible; and who can abide it?

This is a passage that we covered back in chapter five. If you will remember, Joel 2 is a description of the return of the Lord Jesus Christ with His army that parallels what we find in Revelation chapter 19. And this very clearly comes at the end of the Tribulation period – just like Matthew 24 says.

We also find a perfect match for Matthew 24 in Isaiah chapter 13. Once again, we are told that this event takes place at the coming of the Day of the Lord...

*9 Behold, **the day of the Lord cometh,** cruel both with wrath and fierce anger, to lay the land desolate: and he shall destroy the sinners thereof out of it.*

*10 **For the stars of heaven and the constellations thereof shall not give their light: the sun shall be darkened in his going forth, and the moon shall not cause her light to shine.***

11 And I will punish the world for their evil, and the wicked for their iniquity; and I will cause the arrogancy of the proud to cease, and will lay low the haughtiness of the terrible.

12 I will make a man more precious than fine gold; even a man than the golden wedge of Ophir.

13 Therefore I will shake the heavens, and the earth shall remove out of her place, in the wrath of the Lord of hosts, and in the day of his fierce anger.

Can we agree that there is a "match" between Joel 2 and Isaiah 13?

Of course there is a match. It is clear as a bell, and both of them line up perfectly with Matthew 24. In all three instances, there is no light coming from the sun or the moon, and all three of them indicate that this will happen at the coming of the Day of the Lord at the end of the Tribulation period.

Without a doubt, mid-Trib rapture theories make a whole lot more sense than pre-Trib rapture theories, but as you can see they are simply not complete.

As this book has demonstrated over and over, the Bible tells us that the rapture is coming at the end of the Tribulation. Those believers that have already "checked out" on life and are waiting for their ride out of here are going to be bitterly disappointed. We all need to get prepared for what is ahead while there is still time, and we all need to wake up as many of our fellow believers as we can.

As it stands right now, millions of Christians are going to die waiting for a pre-Tribulation rapture or a mid-Tribulation rapture that is never going to come, and that is why it is so imperative that we get this message out to as many of our brothers and sisters in Christ as possible.

-CHAPTER TWENTY FIVE-

A Note Regarding The History Of The Pre-Tribulation Rapture

There is enough material out there about the history of the pre-Tribulation rapture doctrine that one could easily fill up an entire series of books on the topic. As I have been doing research for this book, I have come across an extraordinary amount of information about Margaret MacDonald, the Irvingites, John Darby and the early dispensationalists. I had been urged to really dig into this history and show the corrupt historical roots of this doctrine, but I decided not to do that.

Why?

Well, because you can go back and forth debating all of the historical arguments until the cows come home, but then it always comes back to what the Bible actually says. Even if you can show pre-Tribbers that the concept of a pre-Tribulation rapture was popularized less than 200 years ago by some very questionable people, they will just argue that none of the history really matters anyway because we should just go by what the Bible says. And so in this book I have focused on exactly that.

But for those that do want to learn more about Margaret MacDonald, the Irvingites, John Darby and the early dispensationalists, I would recommend a new video that has been put out by Joe Schimmel of Good Fight Ministries entitled "Left Behind or Led Astray". It is more than two hours long, and it does an outstanding job of dissecting the history of the modern pre-Tribulation rapture movement. I do not intend to try to duplicate his fine work here.

What I will say is that when you study the works of the early church fathers, you find that they make it very clear that the Antichrist will be revealed before the rapture takes place. As noted earlier in this book, this is precisely what Matthew 24 and 2 Thessalonians 2 both say as well.

Let's take a look at just a few examples. The Didache, which many scholars believe was written between AD 50 and AD 70, says the following...

"Watch for your life's sake. Let not your lamps be quenched, nor your loins unloosed; but be ye ready, for ye know not the hour in which our Lord cometh. But often shall ye come together, seeking the things which are befitting to your souls: for the whole time of your faith will not profit you, if ye be not made perfect in the last time. For in the last days false prophets and corrupters shall be multiplied, and the sheep shall be turned into wolves, and love shall be turned into hate; for when lawlessness increaseth, they shall hate and persecute and betray one another, **and then shall appear the world-deceiver as Son of God, and shall do signs and wonders, and the earth shall be delivered into his hands, and he shall do iniquitous things which have never yet come to pass since the beginning.** *Then shall the creation of men come into the fire of trial, and many shall be made to stumble and shall perish; but they that endure in their faith shall be saved from under the curse itself.* **And then shall appear the signs of the truth; first, the sign of an out-spreading in heaven; then the sign of the sound of the trumpet; and the third, the resurrection of the dead;** *yet not of all, but as it is said: The Lord shall come and all His saints with Him. Then shall the world see the Lord coming upon the clouds of heaven." (Chapter XVI)*

Irenaeus (AD 120-202) also taught that the church was going to have to face the wrath of the Antichrist. Here is one example...

"But he [John] indicates the number of the name [Antichrist, 666] now, that when this man comes **we may avoid him, being aware who he is**" *(Against Heresies V, 30, 4).*

And here is another...

"For all these and other words were unquestionably spoken in reference to the resurrection of the just, **which takes place after the coming of Antichrist, and the destruction of all nations under his rule**; *in [the times of] which [resurrection] the righteous shall reign on the earth, waxing stronger by the sight of the Lord: and through Him they shall become accustomed to partake in the glory of God the Father, and shall enjoy in the kingdom intercourse and communion with the holy angels, and union with spiritual beings;* **and those whom the Lord shall find in the flesh, awaiting Him from heaven, and who have suffered tribulation, as well as escaped the hands of the Wicked one**." *(Against Heresies V, XXXV, 1)*

Justin Martyr (AD 100-165) expressed similar sentiments when he wrote the following...

"The man of apostasy [Antichrist], who speaks strange things against the Most High, shall venture to do unlawful deeds on the earth **against US THE CHRISTIANS**..." *(Dialogue With Trypho, 110).*

And Hippolytus (AD 170-236) believed the exact same thing...

*"**Now concerning the tribulation of the persecution which is to fall upon the Church from the adversary**, John also speaks thus, "And I saw a great and wondrous sign in heaven; a woman clothed with the sun, ... And to the woman were given two wings of a great eagle, that she might fly into the wilderness, where she is nourished for a time, and times, and half a time, from the face of the serpent." **That refers to the one thousand two hundred and threescore days (the half of the week) during which the tyrant is to reign and persecute the Church.**... These things then, being come to pass, beloved, and the one week being divided into two parts, and the abomination of desolation being manifested then, and the two prophets and forerunners of the Lord having finished their course, and the whole world finally approaching the consummation, what remains but the coming of our Lord and Saviour Jesus Christ from heaven, for whom we have looked in hope." [Treatise on Christ and Antichrist, 60, 61, 64]*

Tertullian (AD 145-220) was another early church father that was exceedingly clear on the matter...

*"In the Revelation of John, again, the order of these times is spread out to view, which "the souls of the martyrs" are taught to wait for beneath the altar, whilst they earnestly pray to be avenged and judged: (taught, I say, to wait), in order that the world may first drink to the dregs the plagues that await it out of the vials of the angels, and that the city of fornication may receive from the ten kings its deserved doom, **and that the beast Antichrist, with his false prophet may wage war on the Church of God**; and that, after the casting of the devil into the bottomless pit for a while, the blessed prerogative of the first resurrection may be obtained from the thrones; and then again, after the*

consignment of him to the fire, that the judgment of the final and universal resurrection may be determined out of the books. Since, then, the Scriptures both indicate the stages of the last times, and concentrate the harvest of the Christian hope in the very end of the world." [On the Resurrection of the Flesh, XXV]

I could go on and on, but I think that you get the point.

The early church believed that the rapture would come after the Tribulation, and this has been the dominant position all throughout church history, but you won't hear this much in evangelical circles today because it doesn't support the pre-Tribulation position.

However, once again I want to stress that I don't intend to get bogged down in historical debates. Because in the end, whatever people may or may not have believed in the past, and no matter how weird their theological positions may have been, what really matters is what the Bible actually has to say.

And as we have seen throughout this book, the Bible very clearly states that the rapture is coming **after** the Tribulation.

In the next chapter, we will look at some more passages that relate to the timing of the resurrection...

-CHAPTER TWENTY SIX-

On The Last Day

One of the favorite arguments that those that adhere to a post-Tribulation rapture position commonly use comes out of John chapter 6. Four separate times in this chapter, Jesus explains that those who follow Him will be raised up "at the last day"...

John 6:39

*And this is the Father's will which hath sent me, that of all which he hath given me I should lose nothing, but should raise it up again **at the last day**.*

John 6:40

*And this is the will of him that sent me, that every one which seeth the Son, and believeth on him, may have everlasting life: and I will raise him up **at the last day**.*

John 6:44

*No man can come to me, except the Father which hath sent me draw him: and I will raise him up **at the last day**.*

John 6:54

*Whoso eateth my flesh, and drinketh my blood, hath eternal life; and I will raise him up **at the last day**.*

At first glance, those verses certainly seem to be more supportive of a post-Trib position rather than a pre-Trib or mid-Trib position.

But exactly what does "at the last day" mean?

That is a tricky question. In Revelation 20, we are told that the "first resurrection" comes before the thousand year reign of Christ. So there are certainly more "days" after the rapture takes place. In fact, there will be more "days" for a thousand years afterwards.

So why did Jesus use the phrase "at the last day"?

Did He mean the last day of the Tribulation?

Did He mean the last day of this age?

Did He mean the last day before He begins to reign?

There is certainly a lot of room for debate here, and I am going to share with you what I think.

Based on my study of the Scriptures, I believe that "the Day of the Lord" refers to the one thousand year reign of Christ that follows the first six thousand years of human history. So when Jesus says that believers will be resurrected "at the last day", He is referring to the very beginning of the "seventh day" which takes place immediately following the first six "days" of human history.

Let's take a closer look at this. In 2 Peter 3:8, we are told that the Lord considers "a thousand years as one day"...

*But, beloved, be not ignorant of this one thing, **that one day is with the Lord as a thousand years, and a thousand years as one day**.*

Many dismiss this verse as simply being a figure of speech, but I have become convinced that there is something deeper here.

Lending more credence to this theory is Genesis 6:3...

And the LORD said, My spirit shall not always strive with man, for that he also is flesh: yet his days shall be an **hundred and twenty years***.*

The Hebrew word that is translated in this verse as "years" can also be translated other ways as well. This Hebrew word can mean "division of time", "measure of time", and it can be used as an indication of age. And certainly after this passage we read of men living much longer than 120 years.

Personally, I am convinced that this verse is referring to 120 jubilee cycles, which would work out to precisely 6000 years.

And then we also have this prophecy out of Hosea chapter 6...

2 **After two days** *will he revive us: in* **the third day** *he will raise us up, and we shall live in his sight.*

Many believe that this is a prophecy that indicates that the Millennial reign will come exactly two thousand years after the first coming of Christ. Since the first coming of Jesus was about 4000 years from creation, that would put the timing of the fulfillment of this prophecy from Hosea at right around the 6000 year mark.

According to ancient Jewish tradition, Rosh Hashanah (the Feast of Trumpets) is "the birthday of the world". I believe that was the beginning of the "first day", and it is when God's prophetic clock started.

Moving forward 6000 years from that date, it brings us to another Rosh Hashanah, which is exactly when I believe the rapture will take place. And I am also convinced that the seven year Tribulation period will also start on a Rosh Hashanah exactly seven years earlier.

If you have not been exposed to this before, I know that it is a lot to grasp. But this is how God works. He works in cycles and patterns. This is one of the reasons why the Sabbath is celebrated on the seventh day. We do it to remember that God rested on the seventh day of creation, but we also do it to look forward to when Jesus will reign from Jerusalem for a thousand years on the "seventh day" of human history.

So in John chapter 6 if Jesus was saying that the resurrection takes place when "the last day" arrives, that would be the very first day (Rosh Hashanah) of the 6001st year since the creation of the planet. That explanation would be perfectly consistent with everything else that I have written in this book.

Two verses after Peter tells us "that one day is with the Lord as a thousand years, and a thousand years as one day", he gives us a description of what the coming of the Day of the Lord will be like. The following is what 2 Peter 3:10 says...

*But the day of the Lord will come as a thief in the night; in the which **the heavens shall pass away with a great noise**, and the elements shall melt with fervent heat, the earth also and the works that are therein shall be burned up.*

There is another passage in the Bible which also connects the passing away of the heavens to the resurrection of the saints.

In Job chapter 14:12-14, Job makes the following astounding statements...

*12 So man lieth down, and riseth not: **till the heavens be no more**, they shall not awake, nor be raised out of their sleep.*

*13 O that thou wouldest hide me in the grave, that thou wouldest keep me secret, **until thy wrath be past**, that thou wouldest appoint me a set time, and remember me!*

*14 If a man die, shall he live again? all the days of my appointed time will I wait, **till my change come**.*

If the resurrection does not take place "till the heavens be no more", then how in the world could a pre-Trib or a mid-Trib position possibly be accurate?

We find a similar passage in the book of Isaiah. This is what Isaiah 26:19-21 says...

*19 **Thy dead men shall live, together with my dead body shall they arise**. Awake and sing, ye that dwell in dust: for thy dew is as the dew of herbs, and the earth shall cast out the dead.*

20 Come, my people, enter thou into thy chambers, and shut thy doors about thee: hide thyself as it were for a little moment, until the indignation be overpast.

*21 For, behold, **the Lord cometh out of his place to punish the inhabitants of the earth for their iniquity**: the earth also shall disclose her blood, and shall no more cover her slain.*

When does the Lord come "out of His place" to punish the inhabitants of the earth?

This happens when the Lord Jesus returns at the Battle of Armageddon, and this passage in Isaiah seems to link the resurrection of believers (the rapture) with that event.

And of course we have already covered the fact that Revelation chapter 20 tells us that the rapture comes after the Tribulation and at the beginning of the Millennium...

4 And I saw thrones, and they sat upon them, and judgment was given unto them: and I saw the souls of them that were beheaded for the witness of Jesus, and for the word of God, and which had not worshipped the beast, neither his image, neither had received his mark upon their foreheads, or in their hands; and they lived and reigned with Christ a thousand years.

5 But the rest of the dead lived not again until the thousand years were finished. **This is the first resurrection.**

6 Blessed and holy is he that hath part in the first resurrection: on such the second death hath no power, but they shall be priests of God and of Christ, and shall reign with him a thousand years.

I hope that you are starting to see that all of these pieces truly do fit together like a puzzle.

When the seventh trumpet is blown in Revelation 11, it is not just to announce that the rapture has come. It also marks an end of the seven year Tribulation period and the first six thousand years of human history, and it marks the beginning of the Millennial reign (also known in Scripture as "the Day of the Lord" and "the last day"). Let's take a look at Revelation 11:15-18 again...

15 **The seventh angel sounded**, *and there were loud voices in heaven, saying:*

"The kingdoms of the world have become the kingdoms of our Lord, and of His Christ, and He shall reign forever and ever."

16 And the twenty-four elders, who sat before God on their thrones, fell on their faces and worshipped God,

*17 saying: "We give You thanks, O Lord God Almighty, who is and was and who is to come, because You have taken Your great power and **begun to reign**.*

*18 The nations were angry, and **Your wrath has come**, and **the time has come for the dead to be judged**, and **to reward Your servants the prophets and the saints and those who fear Your name**, small and great, and to destroy those who destroy the earth."*

When the seventh trumpet is sounded, several key things happen. The dead are judged, the servants of Christ are rewarded at the rapture, Jesus begins to reign, and God's wrath is unleashed shortly thereafter during the vial judgments. All of this happens immediately after the Tribulation and at the beginning of "the last day". The Biblical festivals of Rosh Hashanah, Yom Kippur and the Feast of Tabernacles give us a prophetic template for how events will subsequently unfold, but most Christians don't even realize this.

When you just allow the Bible to speak for itself, an amazingly consistent picture emerges. But when you try to fit all of these various passages into some sort of pre-conceived notion of what you think they should say, it gets very convoluted very quickly.

God is not trying to trick us. He wants us to know what is going to happen in advance, and He has given us specific signs that must happen before Jesus will return.

In the next chapter, we will examine some more of these signs...

-CHAPTER TWENTY SEVEN-

The Curious Case Of Daniel 12

Did you know that the rapture is in the book of Daniel? In the very last chapter, we find what is perhaps the clearest description of the resurrection in the entire Old Testament...

*And **at that time shall Michael stand up**, the great prince which standeth for the children of thy people: and **there shall be a time of trouble, such as never was since there was a nation even to that same time**: and at that time thy people shall be delivered, every one that shall be found written in the book.*

*2 **And many of them that sleep in the dust of the earth shall awake**, some to everlasting life, and some to shame and everlasting contempt.*

I want you to notice a couple of things here.

First of all, the resurrection follows "a time of trouble" unlike anything the people of God have ever seen before. This sounds so similar to what Jesus said in Matthew 24:21...

21 For then shall be great tribulation, such as was not since the beginning of the world to this time, no, nor ever shall be.

Secondly, I want you to notice that the angel Michael is involved somehow. With that in mind, let's go back and review a couple of verses from 1 Thessalonians 4 once again...

*16 For the Lord himself shall descend from heaven with a shout, **with the voice of the archangel**, and with the trump of God: and the dead in Christ shall rise first:*

17 Then we which are alive and remain shall be caught up together with them in the clouds, to meet the Lord in the air: and so shall we ever be with the Lord.

So precisely who is the archangel?

The book of Jude gives us his identity...

*9 Yet **Michael the archangel**, when contending with the devil he disputed about the body of Moses, durst not bring against him a railing accusation, but said, The Lord rebuke thee.*

So in both 1 Thessalonians 4 and Daniel 12, we see the archangel Michael discussed in conjunction with the rapture. Those that believe in a pre-Tribulation rapture want to place the events of 1 Thessalonians 4 before the rapture, but as we will see, Daniel 12 clearly says that the rapture comes after the Tribulation. Here is the rest of Daniel 12...

3 And they that be wise shall shine as the brightness of the firmament; and they that turn many to righteousness as the stars for ever and ever.

4 But thou, O Daniel, shut up the words, and seal the book, even to the time of the end: many shall run to and fro, and knowledge shall be increased.

5 Then I Daniel looked, and, behold, there stood other two, the one on this side of the bank of the river, and the other on that side of the bank of the river.

*6 And one said to the man clothed in linen, which was upon the waters of the river, **How long shall it be to the end of these wonders?***

*7 And I heard the man clothed in linen, which was upon the waters of the river, when he held up his right hand and his left hand unto heaven, and sware by him that liveth for ever **that it shall be for a time, times, and an half**; and when he shall have accomplished to scatter the power of the holy people, all these things shall be finished.*

*8 And I heard, but I understood not: then said I, O my Lord, **what shall be the end of these things?***

9 And he said, Go thy way, Daniel: for the words are closed up and sealed till the time of the end.

10 Many shall be purified, and made white, and tried; but the wicked shall do wickedly: and none of the wicked shall understand; but the wise shall understand.

*11 **And from the time that the daily sacrifice shall be taken away, and the abomination that maketh desolate set up, there shall be a thousand two hundred and ninety days.***

12 Blessed is he that waiteth, and cometh to the thousand three hundred and five and thirty days.

13 But go thou thy way till the end be: for thou shalt rest, and stand in thy lot at the end of the days.

Daniel, like so many of us, was quite curious about the timing of these things. Perhaps it is just human nature to want to know when the end will come.

In verse 7, Daniel is told that there will be "a time, times and an half" before the resurrection takes place. This seems to correspond to the three and a half years of the second half of the seven year Tribulation period during which the "war on the saints" mentioned in the book of Revelation and elsewhere in Daniel will happen.

In verse 11, Daniel is told that the abomination of desolation begins a stretch of "a thousand two hundred and ninety days". This is a period of time slightly longer than three and a half years on the Hebrew calendar.

Then in verse 12, we are told that those that wait for the end of "the thousand three hundred and five and thirty days" will be blessed.

The difference in those two timeframes has always puzzled those that have studied Bible prophecy, including myself. As with so many other things in Bible prophecy, as that time gets closer I think that it is likely that our understanding will increase.

For now, what I think that we can all agree on is that the abomination of desolation is the starting point for the countdown that Daniel was given, and this should remind you of something that Jesus said in Matthew 24...

15 *When ye therefore shall see* **the abomination of desolation**, *spoken of by Daniel the prophet, stand in the holy place, (whoso readeth, let him understand:)*

16 *Then let them which be in Judaea flee into the mountains:*

17 *Let him which is on the housetop not come down to take any thing out of his house:*

18 *Neither let him which is in the field return back to take his clothes.*

19 And woe unto them that are with child, and to them that give suck in those days!

20 But pray ye that your flight be not in the winter, neither on the sabbath day:

*21 **For then shall be great tribulation**, such as was not since the beginning of the world to this time, no, nor ever shall be.*

And then later on in Matthew 24, we see what happens at the end of this period of great tribulation...

*29 **Immediately after the tribulation of those days** shall the sun be darkened, and the moon shall not give her light, and the stars shall fall from heaven, and the powers of the heavens shall be shaken:*

30 And then shall appear the sign of the Son of man in heaven: and then shall all the tribes of the earth mourn, and they shall see the Son of man coming in the clouds of heaven with power and great glory.

31 And he shall send his angels with a great sound of a trumpet, and they shall gather together his elect from the four winds, from one end of heaven to the other.

In both Daniel 12 and Matthew 24, the abomination of desolation starts off a period of great tribulation unlike anything the world has ever seen before. Daniel tells us that this period of time will last for approximately three and a half years, and both Daniel and Matthew tell us that the rapture of God's people will take place after the time of tribulation is over.

All of the passages about the end times that we find in the Bible are telling us the same thing. Our Father wants us to know what to watch for as we approach the return of His Son, and that is why there is so much material in the Word of God about these things. If we refuse to allow man-made theories and opinions to cloud our thinking, what the Bible says about the last days is actually very clear. We just need to be careful not to let our pride get in the way of what He is trying to show us.

-CHAPTER TWENTY EIGHT-

Every Eye Will See Him

Those that believe that the Lord will come back for His bride before the Tribulation begins typically promote a concept known as "the secret rapture". This theory has been promoted by countless books and movies, and it is now believed by tens of millions of believers around the globe. Essentially, the idea is that when "the secret rapture" occurs, vast numbers of Christians will instantly disappear without a trace and everyone else will have no idea what just happened to them. There will be no noise, no fanfare and nobody will see Jesus in the clouds.

But is this really what the Bible says?

In Revelation 1:7, we are told that "every eye shall see him" at his coming...

Behold, he cometh with clouds; **and every eye shall see him***, and they also which pierced him: and all kindreds of the earth shall wail because of him. Even so, Amen.*

If you will remember, clouds are also mentioned in Matthew 24, 1 Thessalonians 4 and Revelation 14. Every other passage where it mentions Jesus coming with the clouds is speaking of the rapture, and so those that want to put Revelation 1:7 into a different category are really facing an uphill battle.

Many pre-Tribbers like to repeat the mantra that Jesus is coming "as a thief in the night", and this is something that we covered in a previous chapter. But just because Jesus is coming as a thief does not mean that it will be a quiet event. Just check out what 2 Peter 3:10 has to say about the matter...

*10 But the day of the Lord will come **as a thief in the night**; in the which the heavens shall pass away **with a great noise**, and the elements shall melt **with fervent heat**, the earth also and the works that are therein shall be burned up.*

I don't know about you, but that sounds rather tumultuous to me.

Luke 17 is another place where the coming of the Lord is portrayed as something much different than a "secret". This is what Luke 17:24 says...

24 For as the lightning, that lighteneth out of the one part under heaven, shineth unto the other part under heaven; so shall also the Son of man be in his day.

And we know that Jesus is talking about the rapture here, because this is what we find just a few short verses later...

34 I tell you, in that night there shall be two men in one bed; the one shall be taken, and the other shall be left.

35 Two women shall be grinding together; the one shall be taken, and the other left.

36 Two men shall be in the field; the one shall be taken, and the other left.

If you are thinking that this sounds very similar to Matthew 24, you would be quite correct. As we have covered earlier in this book, Matthew 24 is very clearly speaking of the rapture, and once again we see that there is not going to be anything "quiet" or "secret" about it whatsoever...

*27 For as the lightning cometh out of the east, and shineth even unto the west; so shall also the coming ("**parousia**") of the Son of man be.*

28 For wheresoever the carcase is, there will the eagles be gathered together.

29 Immediately after the tribulation of those days shall the sun be darkened, and the moon shall not give her light, and the stars shall fall from heaven, and the powers of the heavens shall be shaken:

30 And then shall appear the sign of the Son of man in heaven: and then shall all the tribes of the earth mourn, and they shall see the Son of man coming in the clouds of heaven with power and great glory.

31 And he shall send his angels with a great sound of a trumpet, and they shall gather together his elect from the four winds, from one end of heaven to the other.

So all of those movies that you have seen where people wake up to find neatly folded piles of clothing next to them are all dead wrong.

When Jesus comes back for His bride, the entire world is going to know about it.

Unfortunately, most Christians have been so conditioned to think differently about the rapture that it is very difficult for many of them to imagine it happening as the Bible actually describes.

That is why books such as this one are going to be so important in the years ahead. Believers deserve to know the truth about the rapture, and those that are teaching a secret pre-Tribulation rapture need to stop misleading the flock.

-CHAPTER TWENTY NINE-

People Are Going To Be Angry

In America today, there are millions upon millions of Christians that believe in a pre-Tribulation rapture with all of their hearts. Many of them were taught to believe in a pre-Tribulation rapture from early childhood on up, and some have never even been presented with any other possibility. Their pastors taught it to them, all of the Bible prophecy books that they have ever read boldly proclaimed that it would happen, and an endless parade of high profile experts have assured them that Christians are not going to have to face the chaos that we see in the book of Revelation.

So how are all of those people going to feel when they realize that they have been duped and that they are going to have to go through the Tribulation after all?

I believe that we are going to see anger on a level that we have never seen in the church ever before. Like I said at the beginning of this book, there are a whole lot of people out there that are making major life decisions based on this doctrine. When there is no pre-Tribulation rapture, I am convinced that many extremely angry believers will seek to confront the pastors and teachers that led them astray. I fear that some of these confrontations may be violent.

Others will completely give in to depression and despair. Because they are totally unprepared for what is coming, many will feel like they have absolutely no hope left. Let us pray that it does not happen, but we may actually see some Christians choose to take their lives rather than face hell on earth.

And of course there is the possibility that some may choose to abandon their faith altogether. I grew up around churches and ministries that fully embraced the doctrine of a pre-Tribulation rapture, and so I know how central it is to the faith of many. For millions upon millions of Christians, it really is at the very core of what they believe.

So once that is stripped away from them, will they question everything else that they have been taught to believe as well?

Don't think that it can't happen. Over the years, I have seen so many believers that I thought were very solid fall away for one reason or another. And the Scriptures do warn us that there will be a great falling away before the rapture finally takes place (2 Thessalonians 2:3).

Without a doubt, the mockers are going to have a field day in the years ahead. When global events start spinning out of control and everyone starts saying that the Tribulation is here, the mocking of those that believe in a pre-Tribulation rapture is going to reach epic proportions. Of course this was prophesied nearly 2000 years ago by the Apostle Peter. This is what 2 Peter 3:3-4 says...

*3 Knowing this first, **that there shall come in the last days scoffers**, walking after their own lusts,*

*4 And saying, **Where is the promise of his coming?** for since the fathers fell asleep, all things continue as they were from the beginning of the creation.*

Are we living in the last days?

Of course we are.

So this passage is for our time.

Yes, there are already those that mock the idea of the second coming of our Lord and Savior Jesus Christ, but I believe that this is going to get much, much worse in the years ahead, especially once it becomes evident that no pre-Tribulation rapture is going to take place.

Any Christian leader that chooses to teach about the events of the last days and the timing of the rapture is taking on a great deal of responsibility.

If you are one of these leaders, you should know that people are making decisions on whether or not to get prepared based on what you are telling them.

As it stands, there are millions upon millions of believers that are utterly unprepared physically, mentally, emotionally and spiritually for what is ahead.

With God's help, we can make it through the hard times and persecution that are coming. But if people are only given the message that they are going to get pulled out of here before anything really bad happens, they are going to be completely blindsided by the storm that is rapidly approaching.

Here is something else to think about. If believers have had it pounded into their heads that the rapture has to come before the Tribulation, how will they respond when the Mark of the Beast shows up?

Could it be possible that some of them will end up taking it, thinking that there is no way that it could actually be "the Mark" because the rapture has not happened yet?

Like I said, those that teach on Christian eschatology bear great responsibility.

If you do not handle the Word of God with care, you could end up with blood on your hands.

The doctrine of the pre-Tribulation rapture could also cause many to completely miss out on their God-given destinies.

It is my conviction that the greatest move of God that the world has ever seen will happen at some point between right now and the return of our Lord and Savior. But many Christians don't want to hear anything about the great move of God that is coming, because they believe that their time on this planet is just about done.

As I discussed earlier in this book, it is as if these believers are at the party of a lifetime, but they are missing all of the action because they are spending the entire time waiting by the front door for their rides to show up.

For so many years, a lot of highly respected Bible teachers have avoided confronting the false doctrine of the pre-Tribulation rapture because they didn't want to alienate people.

But the truth is that what people believe about the rapture really matters.

The seeds that are being planted right now are going to have very serious consequences in the years ahead. So much of the anguish, despair and confusion that we are going to witness could have been avoided if Christian leaders had been honest with their flocks.

Nowhere in the Bible does it say that there is going to be a pre-Tribulation rapture. If you are a Christian leader and you still find yourself holding on to a belief in a pre-Trib rapture after reading this book, at least be honest with those under your care. Please let them know that there are other possibilities, and that they need to do their own research and come to their own conclusions.

Those that are boldly assuring believers that they will be swept away by "the blessed hope" before the trials of the Great Tribulation are doing a great amount of damage to the body of Christ. The damage may not be very visible right now, but during the hard years to come it is going to become exceedingly apparent.

For the moment, debates about the timing of the rapture may be considered to be an "intellectual exercise" by some, but the cold, hard reality of the matter is that what people believe about the rapture is going to have tremendous consequences moving forward.

Hopefully this book is helping you to grasp what is at stake. The fate of millions could literally be hanging in the balance. So don't let your pride stand in the way of seeing the truth.

-CHAPTER THIRTY-

Corrie Ten Boom's Ominous Warning

Corrie Ten Boom is a legend in the Christian world, and she knew a thing or two about Christian persecution. During World War II, her family helped hide Jewish families that were attempting to escape the Nazi Holocaust. As a result, her entire family was arrested, and she was hauled off to a Nazi concentration camp. She survived, but her sister did not. Eventually she went on to write *The Hiding Place*, which ultimately sold more than two million copies worldwide.

In this chapter, I want to share with you a letter that Corrie Ten Boom wrote in 1974 regarding the doctrine of the pre-Tribulation rapture. I think that this is a letter that needs to be read by all Christians today, and so I have reproduced it in its entirety...

*****

The world is deathly ill. It is dying. The Great Physician has already signed the death certificate. Yet there is still a great work for Christians to do. They are to be streams of living water, channels of mercy to those who are still in the world. It is possible for them to do this because they are overcomers.

Christians are ambassadors for Christ. They are representatives from Heaven to this dying world. And because of our presence here, things will change.

My sister, Betsy, and I were in the Nazi concentration camp at Ravensbruck because we committed the crime of loving Jews. Seven hundred of us from Holland, France, Russia, Poland and Belgium were herded into a room built for two hundred. As far as I knew, Betsy and I were the only two representatives of Heaven in that room.

We may have been the Lord's only representatives in that place of hatred, yet because of our presence there, things changed. Jesus said, "In the world you shall have tribulation; but be of good cheer, I have overcome the world" (John 16:33) We too, are to be overcomers – bringing the light of Jesus into a world filled with darkness and hate.

Sometimes I get frightened as I read the Bible, and as I look in this world and see all of the tribulation and persecution promised by the Bible coming true. Now I can tell you, though, if you too are afraid, that I have just read the last pages. I can now come to shouting "Hallelujah! Hallelujah!" for I have found where it is written that Jesus said,

"He that overcomes shall inherit all things: and I will be His God, and he shall be My son." (Revelation 21:7)

This is the future and hope of this world. Not that the world will survive – but that we shall be overcomers in the midst of a dying world.

Betsy and I, in the concentration camp, prayed that God would heal Betsy who was so weak and sick.

"Yes, the Lord will heal me," Betsy said with confidence.

She died the next day and I could not understand it. They laid her thin body on the concrete floor along with all the other corpses of the women who died that day.

It was hard for me to understand, to believe that God had a purpose for all that. Yet because of Betsy's death, today I am traveling all over the world telling people about Jesus.

There are some among us teaching there will be no tribulation, that the Christians will be able to escape all this. These are the false teachers that Jesus was warning us to expect in the latter days. Most of them have little knowledge of what is already going on across the world. I have been in countries where the saints are already suffering terrible persecution.

In China, the Christians were told, "Don't worry, before the tribulation comes you will be translated – raptured." Then came a terrible persecution. Millions of Christians were tortured to death. Later I heard a Bishop from China say, sadly,

"We have failed. We should have made the people strong for persecution, rather than telling them Jesus would come first. Tell the people how to be strong in times of persecution, how to stand when the tribulation comes, to stand and not faint."

I feel I have a divine mandate to go and tell the people of this world that it is possible to be strong in the Lord Jesus Christ. We are in training for the tribulation, but more than sixty percent of the Body of Christ across the world has already entered into the tribulation. There is no way to escape it. We are next.

Since I have already gone through prison for Jesus' sake, and since I met the Bishop in China, now every time I read a good Bible text I think, "Hey, I can use that in the time of tribulation." Then I write it down and learn it by heart.

When I was in the concentration camp, a camp where only twenty percent of the women came out alive, we tried to cheer each other up by saying, "Nothing could be any worse than today." But we would find the next day was even worse.

During this time a Bible verse that I had committed to memory gave me great hope and joy.

If you are reviled for the name of Christ, you are blessed, because the Spirit of glory and of God rests on you. Make sure that none of you suffers as a murderer, or thief, or evildoer, or a troublesome meddler; but if anyone suffers as a Christian, he is not to be ashamed, but is to glorify God in this name. (1 Peter 4:14-15)

I found myself saying, "Hallelujah! Because I am suffering (for the name of Christ), Jesus is glorified!"

In America, the churches sing, "Let the congregation escape tribulation", but in China and Africa the tribulation has already arrived. This last year alone more than two hundred thousand Christians were martyred in Africa. Now things like that never get into the newspapers because they cause bad political relations. But I know. I have been there. We need to think about that when we sit down in our nice houses with our nice clothes to eat our steak dinners. Many, many members of the Body of Christ are being tortured to death at this very moment, yet we continue right on as though we are all going to escape the tribulation.

Several years ago I was in Africa in a nation where a new government had come into power. The first night I was there some of the Christians were commanded to come to the police station to register. When they arrived they were arrested and that same night they were executed. The next day the same thing happened with other Christians. The third day it was the same. All the Christians in the district were being systematically murdered.

The fourth day I was to speak in a little church. The people came, but they were filled with fear and tension. All during the service they were looking at each other, their eyes asking, "Will this one I am sitting beside be the next one killed? Will I be the next one?"

The room was hot and stuffy with insects that came through the screenless windows and swirled around the naked bulbs over the bare wooden benches. I told them a story out of my childhood.

"When I was a little girl, I went to my father and said, "Daddy, I am afraid that I will never be strong enough to be a martyr for Jesus Christ."

"Tell me," said Father, "When you take a train trip to Amsterdam, when do I give you the money for the ticket? Three weeks before?"

"No, Daddy, you give me the money for the ticket just before we get on the train."

"That is right," my father said, "and so it is with God's strength. Our Father in Heaven knows when you will need the strength to be a martyr for Jesus Christ. He will supply all you need, just in time."

My African friends were nodding and smiling. Suddenly a spirit of joy descended upon that church and the people began singing, "In the sweet, by and by, we shall meet on that beautiful shore."

Later that week, half the congregation of that church was executed. I heard later that the other half was killed some months ago.

But I must tell you something. I was so happy that the Lord used me to encourage these people, for unlike many of their leaders, I had the word of God. I had been to the Bible and discovered that Jesus said He had not only overcome the world, but to all those who remained faithful to the end, He would give a crown of life.

How can we get ready for the persecution?

First we need to feed on the Word of God, digest it, and make it a part of our being. This will mean disciplined Bible study each day as we not only memorize long passages of scripture, but put the principles to work in our lives.

Next we need to develop a personal relationship with Jesus Christ. Not just the Jesus of yesterday, the Jesus of History, but the life-changing Jesus of today who is still alive and sitting at the right hand of God.

We must be filled with the Holy Spirit. This is not an optional command of the Bible, it is absolutely necessary. Those earthly disciples could never have stood up under the persecution of the Jews and Romans had they not waited for Pentecost. Each of us needs our own personal Pentecost, the baptism of the Holy Spirit. We will never be able to stand in the tribulation without it.

In the coming persecution we must be ready to help each other and encourage each other. But we must not wait until the tribulation comes before starting. The fruit of the Spirit should be the dominant force of every Christian's life.

Many are fearful of the coming tribulation. They want to run. I, too, am a little bit afraid when I think that after all my eighty years, including the horrible Nazi concentration camp that I might have to go through the tribulation also. But then I read the Bible and I am glad.

When I am weak, then I shall be strong, the Bible says. Betsy and I were prisoners for the Lord, we were so weak, but we got power because the Holy Spirit was on us. That mighty inner strengthening of the Holy Spirit helped us through. No, you will not be strong in yourself when the tribulation comes. Rather, you will be strong in the power of Him who will not forsake you. For seventy-six years I have known the Lord Jesus and not once has He ever left me, or let me down.

Though He slay me, I will hope in Him. (Job 13:15)

I know that to all who overcome, He shall give the crown of life. Hallelujah!

– Corrie Ten Boom – 1974

-CHAPTER THIRTY ONE-

The Tribulation Is Not Starting Yet

As global events spiral out of control over the next few years, it is going to become very popular to say that we have already entered the seven year Tribulation period. In fact, there are already a few people out there that are going around telling people that we are already in the Great Tribulation.

But the truth, of course, is that the Tribulation has not started yet, nor are we about to enter that period of time.

There are still certain things that must happen before the Tribulation begins. One of them is the rise of the ten-horned one world government that is described in the book of Daniel and the book of Revelation.

In Daniel 7:19-25, we find that this ten-horned one world government arises **before** the Antichrist comes on the scene...

19 Then I would know the truth of the fourth beast, which was diverse from all the others, exceeding dreadful, whose teeth were of iron, and his nails of brass; which devoured, brake in pieces, and stamped the residue with his feet;

20 And of the ten horns that were in his head, and of the other which came up, and before whom three fell; even of that horn that had eyes, and a mouth that spake very great things, whose look was more stout than his fellows.

21 I beheld, and the same horn made war with the saints, and prevailed against them;

22 Until the Ancient of days came, and judgment was given to the saints of the most High; and the time came that the saints possessed the kingdom.

23 Thus he said, The fourth beast shall be the fourth kingdom upon earth, which shall be diverse from all kingdoms, and shall devour the whole earth, and shall tread it down, and break it in pieces.

24 And the ten horns out of this kingdom are ten kings that shall arise: **and another shall rise after them;** *and he shall be diverse from the first, and he shall subdue three kings.*

25 And he shall speak great words against the most High, and shall wear out the saints of the most High, and think to change times and laws: and they shall be given into his hand until a time and times and the dividing of time.

So do you see the order there?

The one world government comes first, and then the Antichrist is given power over it later.

Another thing that we are watching for is the rebuilding of the Jewish temple in Jerusalem. This has to be completed by the midpoint of the Tribulation period so that the Antichrist can commit the "abomination of desolation" mentioned in Matthew 24.

Another place this is discussed is in 2 Thessalonians 2. I know that we have used this passage repeatedly in this book, but it is critical that you see this. Until the temple has been rebuilt, 2 Thessalonians 2:1-4 cannot be fulfilled...

Now we beseech you, brethren, by the coming of our Lord Jesus Christ, and by our gathering together unto him,

2 That ye be not soon shaken in mind, or be troubled, neither by spirit, nor by word, nor by letter as from us, as that the day of Christ is at hand.

3 Let no man deceive you by any means: for that day shall not come, except there come a falling away first, and that man of sin be revealed, the son of perdition;

4 Who opposeth and exalteth himself above all that is called God, or that is worshipped; **so that he as God sitteth in the temple of God, shewing himself that he is God.**

So if we are not in the Tribulation yet, and it is not about to begin, where are we in the prophetic timeline right now?

Well, I believe that we are in a period of time that was described by the Lord Jesus as "the beginnings of sorrows". In Mark 13:5-8, we find the following...

5 And Jesus answering them began to say, Take heed lest any man deceive you:

6 For many shall come in my name, saying, I am Christ; and shall deceive many.

7 And when ye shall hear of wars and rumours of wars, be ye not troubled: for such things must needs be; but the end shall not be yet.

8 For nation shall rise against nation, and kingdom against kingdom: and there shall be earthquakes in divers places, and there shall be famines and troubles: these are the beginnings of sorrows.

I am convinced that we are standing at the precipice of great global chaos. I believe that we are entering a time of worldwide economic collapse, unprecedented governmental shaking, widespread civil unrest, rapidly rising crime, and an explosion of Islamic terrorism unlike anything we have ever seen before.

I also believe that we are about to see natural disasters on a scale not seen since the days of Noah's flood, a great war in the Middle East following the establishment of a Palestinian state (some refer to this as the Psalm 83 war), and a conflict between the United States and Russia that will shock the entire planet. All of these events taken together will constitute the "perfect storm" that John Paul Jackson and others have warned is coming.

The period of time that we are moving into is going to be even worse than what most Christians imagine the Great Tribulation will be like.

But it won't actually be the Great Tribulation. Instead, it will just be setting the stage for the one world economic system, the one world government, the one world religion and the rise of the one known as the Antichrist.

Right now, the United States is the head of the global system, but that is about to completely change. This is something that I am going to cover in the next chapter...

-CHAPTER THIRTY TWO-

The Judgment Of God Is Coming To America

Years ago, I used to work as an attorney. And in the legal world, a pronouncement of guilt always precedes the administration of justice. For instance, before a criminal defendant begins serving a prison sentence, he is found guilty by a court of law. I believe that something similar has been happening to America as a whole. I am truly convinced that 2015 was a year when we were shown our guilt in unprecedented ways.

One example of this was the Supreme Court decision that legalized gay marriage in all 50 states. The highest court in the land defiled the institution of marriage and permanently established something that God says is morally wrong as a "fundamental right", and a solid majority of the population cheered. The White House, California's capitol building in Sacramento, the Empire State Building and the new World Trade Center tower were all lit up in rainbow colors to celebrate this "achievement". This Supreme Court decision made front page headlines all over the planet, and so the entire world got to see our shame.

Another example of this phenomenon was when the adultery website Ashley Madison got hacked. It turns out that millions of American men were using the site, including hundreds of Christian ministers. But perhaps we shouldn't have been so surprised. A survey conducted by the Barna Group in 2014 discovered that 55 percent of all married Christian men look at pornography at least monthly, and 35 percent of them have had an extra-marital affair. The body of Christ in the United States is incredibly sick, and we are getting more evidence of this all the time.

But perhaps the most striking example of how we were shown our guilt has to do with abortion. During 2015, the Center for Medical Progress released a series of undercover videos that were taken at Planned Parenthood clinics nationwide. The things that were revealed in these videos are almost too horrible to put into words. These videos showed the entire world that we are killing millions of babies, chopping them up into little pieces and harvesting their organs. Once the organs are harvested, they are sold off to the highest bidder, and most of those organs end up being used in bizarre scientific experiments.

After most of these videos had already been released, a survey was taken which asked the American people whether or not we should continue to give federal funding to Planned Parenthood. The results were absolutely astounding.

According to USA Today, 65 percent of all Americans wanted to keep giving hundreds of millions of tax dollars to Planned Parenthood each year, and only 29 percent of all Americans wanted to cut off the funding.

It is important to keep in mind that they were not being asked if Planned Parenthood should be shut down. The only thing that they were being asked was whether or not they should keep getting hundreds of millions of our tax dollars. In one recent year, Planned Parenthood got a total of 553 million dollars from the federal government.

When I saw that only 29 percent of all Americans wanted to end federal funding for Planned Parenthood, I came to one inescapable conclusion.

America is done.

America is finished, and now all that is left is to face judgment.

If we can't even agree that harvesting baby parts and selling them for profit is evil, what hope is there for us as a nation?

I believe that it was no accident that those undercover Planned Parenthood videos came out exactly when they did. God was showing us our sin, and I believe that we were being given one last chance to repent. But instead of repenting, our nation continues to race after even more evil.

Just like Nazi Germany, the beauty and pageantry of our society masks great wickedness. Since Roe v. Wade was decided in 1973, more than 57 million babies have been slaughtered in America. Some estimates put that number closer to 70 million. The blood of tens of millions of babies is crying out for justice, and justice is coming.

I believe that 2015 was a year when America was pronounced guilty. Now the judgment of God is coming, and we are going to deserve every ounce of what is about to happen to us.

As I mentioned in the last chapter, I believe that we are on the verge of entering the "perfect storm" that John Paul Jackson and others have warned about. Our government and our economy will be shaken like never before. Our cities will soon descend into utter chaos. The thin veneer of civilization that we all take for granted will disappear.

In addition to internal threats, we will also be facing Islamic terror on a scale that we have never seen before, a great war will eventually erupt in the Middle East, and down the road the United States will face military conflict with both Russia and China.

And on top of everything else, the U.S. is going to be hit by a series of horrific natural disasters that includes giant earthquakes, unprecedented volcanic eruptions and tsunamis that are almost unimaginable.

By the time it is all over, millions upon millions of Americans will die, and the United States as we know it will cease to exist.

If we would have obeyed God and followed His ways, things would have turned out very, very differently.

But we kept shaking our fist at God as a nation, and we somehow convinced ourselves that there would never be any consequences.

I know that the things that I have covered in this chapter are very hard to hear. Without a doubt, they are also very hard to write. But it isn't going to do any of us any good to hide from the truth.

The American people need to be warned about what is coming, but most churches in this country absolutely refuse to talk about these things. Most churches have become extremely politically correct and are overly concerned about potentially offending people, and meanwhile our nation is steamrolling toward oblivion.

But it isn't all bad news that is on the horizon.

Even in the midst of all the chaos and darkness, God is at work. If you are a Christian, the years that are ahead of us are going to be a wonderful time to be alive.

The greatest move of God that the world has ever seen is coming, and that is something that I am going to talk about in the next chapter...

-CHAPTER THIRTY THREE-

The Remnant Is Rising

Do you want to be part of the Remnant of the last days?

If you are like most believers, the answer to that question is obvious. After all, who wouldn't want to be on the cutting edge of what God is doing in these times? There is a common perception among God's people that God is starting to do something really BIG, and I have found that Christians in the western world are hungry to be part of something that is real and authentic.

But exactly what is the Remnant? There are dozens of pastors, teachers, evangelists and radio hosts that are running around using this term today, and very few of them ever take the time to define it for us.

My definition for "the Remnant" comes directly out of the Bible. Nearly two thousand years ago, the Apostle John prophesied about a group of believers that would exist during the Great Tribulation. This is what Revelation 12:17 says...

*And the dragon was wroth with the woman, and went to make war with **the remnant** of her seed, **which keep the commandments of God, and have the testimony of Jesus Christ**.*

A lot of people like to speculate about what God will or will not do in the last days. But nobody needs to speculate when it comes to the group of believers described here. The Apostle John clearly tells us that these Christians "which keep the commandments of God" and "have the testimony of Jesus Christ" will exist in the last days.

And in case we missed it the first time, this exact same group of believers is mentioned just two chapters later. This is what Revelation 14:12 says...

*Here is the patience of the saints: here are they **that keep the commandments of God, and the faith of Jesus**.*

This is the foundation for my definition of "the Remnant". I believe that God is raising up a Remnant that will keep His commandments, that will bring in the greatest harvest of souls the world has ever seen, and that will move in the power of the Holy Spirit in ways that we have not seen since the first century. God is in the process of restoring all things, and we are going to be the generation that finally gets things right. The greatest move of God of all time is going to happen right before the return of our Lord and Savior Jesus Christ, and we are going to become the kind of bride that He deserves. On our own, this is impossible, but with Him all things are possible.

For a few moments, let's take a closer look at some of the characteristics of the Remnant. In Revelation 12:17 and Revelation 14:12, we are told that they will "keep the commandments of God". That is not something that most Christians in the western world like to hear. We have all become so obsessed with "avoiding legalism" that many of us no longer want to hear anything about holiness at all. And those involved in the "hyper-grace movement" take this to dangerous extremes. There are actually a whole bunch of preachers out there today that are proclaiming that we shouldn't even bother trying to live holy lives because God is already as pleased with us as He ever possibly could be. They derisively dismiss efforts at holy living as "sin management", and they consider repentance to be a waste of time. They believe that God doesn't even see when we commit sin, and therefore we should just relax and live our lives without worrying about whether we are "pleasing God" or not.

The people who fall for this kind of preaching obviously do not know their Bibles. Just look at the messages that Jesus had for the churches in the first three chapters of the book of Revelation. Throughout the New Testament, God calls us to holy living, and He intends for us to keep His commandments. Just read Matthew 5:17-19. Most of the time Jesus spoke in parables, and to this day many of the things that He had to say were a bit puzzling. But there were other times when Jesus spoke very, very clearly, and Matthew 5 is one of those passages. In particular, Jesus did not leave any wiggle room at all in verse 19.

Of course we are not saved by keeping God's commandments. The truth is that we all fall short, and the commandments show us our need for a Savior. In 1 John 3:4, we find that sin is defined as breaking God's commandments, and in Romans 3:20 we are told that "the knowledge of sin" comes through the Law. In other words, God's commandments are a mirror that shows us how dirty we are and how desperately we need the blood of Jesus.

There is nothing that we could ever do to "earn" our salvation. As Romans 3:28 tells us, we are justified by faith in Jesus Christ.

But does that mean that once we are saved we can throw out God's commandments and do whatever we want?

Many churches today would answer "yes" to that question, but in Romans 3:31 the Apostle Paul answers that question with a resounding no. God wants us to keep His commandments, and as we just saw, keeping His commandments will be one of the hallmarks of the Remnant in the last days.

Another key trait of the Remnant is "the testimony of Jesus Christ". We live at a time when multitudes of believers in the western world are ashamed to share the gospel of Jesus Christ publicly. In fact, studies have found that the vast majority of all believers have never led a single person to the Lord.

But the Bible tells us that a great harvest of souls in coming. In the last days, the gospel will be preached "unto all nations", and the Great Commission will finally be fulfilled. Just check out Matthew 24:14...

*And this gospel of the kingdom **shall be preached in all the world for a witness unto all nations**; and **then shall the end come**.*

The Lord Jesus promised us that just before "the end" comes, the message of the cross will be preached "in all the world" and it will be "a witness unto all nations". The world "all" is used twice here, and I believe that He was trying to make a point.

We are finally going to get the job done, and we are going to see a wave of salvation that is absolutely unprecedented in human history just before Jesus comes back.

But of course in order to do this job, we are going to need the power of the Holy Spirit. And in the book of Joel, we find that God tells us that there will be a great outpouring of His Spirit just before "the great and terrible day of the Lord" comes. This is what Joel 2:28-32 says...

*28 And it shall come to pass afterward, that **I will pour out my spirit upon all flesh**; and your sons and your* *daughters shall prophesy, your old men shall dream dreams, your young men shall see visions:*

*29 And also upon the servants and upon the handmaids in those days **will I pour out my spirit**.*

30 And I will shew wonders in the heavens and in the earth, blood, and fire, and pillars of smoke.

*31 The sun shall be turned into darkness, and the moon into blood, **before the great and terrible day of the Lord come**.*

*32 And it shall come to pass, that whosoever shall call on the name of the Lord shall be delivered: for in mount Zion and in Jerusalem shall be deliverance, as the Lord hath said, and in **the remnant** whom the Lord shall call.*

The outpouring of the Holy Spirit that is coming is going to eclipse anything that any of us have ever seen or experienced. In fact, I believe that we are on the precipice of the greatest move of God in all of human history.

And the rise of the Remnant of the last days that I have been talking about in this chapter is not something that will start to happen in the future.

The truth is that it is happening right now.

All over the world, the Remnant is rising, and there is no single individual, ministry, denomination or organization in charge. It is an organic move of God, and it is truly a worldwide phenomenon. All over the planet believers are waking up to these things, and we are seeing the literal fulfillment of what the Apostle John prophesied nearly 2000 years ago.

Of course just because we know about what God is doing does not mean that we automatically get to participate. My wife and I are constantly praying and asking God to allow us to be part of what He is doing in these last days. We want to do what He created us to do, and we don't want to miss out on any part of the destiny that He has planned for us. One thing that we have very clearly learned over time is that God's plan is far superior to our own, and we can't wait to see what He has in store for us next.

As I close this chapter, I want to ask you a question.

What kind of bride does Jesus deserve?

Just think about that for a few moments. Jesus doesn't deserve just a "good" bride. He deserves the very best bride of all. He deserves a bride that is wildly and madly and passionately in love with Him. He deserves a bride that is absolutely obsessed with Him and His Kingdom.

In Ephesians 5:27, we are told that Jesus is coming back for a bride that is without spot or wrinkle...

That he might present it to himself a glorious church, not having spot, or wrinkle, or any such thing; but that it should be holy and without blemish.

Does this describe the church today?

Of course not.

We are going to need the refining fire of the Great Tribulation to purify ourselves. The lukewarm, half-hearted Christianity that pervades so many of our churches and denominations today has got to go.

Jesus deserves a bride that is completely and totally on fire for Him. He doesn't want a bride that is full of compromise and that is addicted to the pleasures of this world. He wants a bride that is entirely consumed with love for Him.

As I stated earlier, we cannot become this kind of bride on our own. We have got to have the help of the Holy Spirit. That is why holiness is so critical. If we are living in sin, the Spirit of God will not move in our lives.

Every great revival begins with repentance, and now is the time to turn to the Lord our God with all of our hearts. We need to be in His Word and in prayer like never before. We need to get rid of anything that is holding us back, and we need to pursue Him with everything that we have got inside of us. In Jeremiah 29:13, we are told the following...

*And ye shall seek me, and find me, when ye shall search for me **with all your heart.***

Now is the time. This generation will see the greatest move of God and the greatest harvest of souls in all of human history. You were born for such a time as this, and your future can be greater than you ever imagined that it could possibly be, but you have got to give everything to Jesus.

So I say to the Remnant – Arise!

The restoration of all things has come, and the bridegroom stands at the door.

If you have been searching for something that will bring meaning to your life, you just found it. The God who created all things loves you immensely, and He has a destiny for your life that is far greater than anything you may have ever dreamed was possible. The war between the kingdom of light and the kingdom of darkness is coming to an end, and we are right at the center of it. In this hour the eternal destiny of billions of souls will be determined, and we are going to write the final chapter of the history of God's people.

If you feel the Holy Spirit prompting you right now, come and join us. Come and join the Remnant. Come and join the army of the last days. We are going to be the generation that finally fulfills the Great Commission and we are going to be the generation that prepares the way for the most dramatic moment in human history – the return of Jesus Christ to this planet.

In the very last chapter in the entire Bible, there is an invitation to those that are searching. This is what Revelation 22:17 says...

*And the Spirit and **the bride** say, **"Come!"** And let him who hears say, **"Come!"** And let him who thirsts come. Whoever desires, let him take the water of life freely.*

You don't have to join any church or denomination or ministry to be a part of the Remnant.

All you have to do is to give everything that you have to the Lord Jesus Christ.

He is coming back for a bride that is completely and totally on fire for Him.

Will you answer the call?

The Spirit and the bride say "Come!"

-CHAPTER THIRTY FOUR-

The Remnant Has Somewhere To Go

Because most evangelical Christians in the western world believe in a pre-Tribulation or mid-Tribulation rapture, most of them don't realize that there will be a place of protection for believers during the second half of the Tribulation period. Jesus tells us about this place of protection in Matthew 24...

15 When ye therefore shall see the abomination of desolation, spoken of by Daniel the prophet, stand in the holy place, (whoso readeth, let him understand:)

*16 **Then let them which be in Judaea flee into the mountains***:

17 Let him which is on the housetop not come down to take any thing out of his house:

18 Neither let him which is in the field return back to take his clothes.

19 And woe unto them that are with child, and to them that give suck in those days!

20 But pray ye that your flight be not in the winter, neither on the sabbath day:

*21 **For then shall be great tribulation, such as was not since the beginning of the world to this time, no, nor ever shall be***.

As we have already covered, the abomination of desolation occurs in the middle of the Tribulation period, and once it takes place Jesus says that those that are living in the land of Israel are to flee to the mountains. Please note that He did not say "just hold on a minute, because I am about to come

get you". If the rapture was coming in the middle of the Tribulation period, you might expect Him to say something like that. But instead, he warns us to flee to the mountains without even taking the time to pack anything.

In Revelation 12:1-6, we are told more about this place of protection. In this passage it is revealed that we will be protected there for 1,260 days...

And there appeared a great wonder in heaven; a woman clothed with the sun, and the moon under her feet, and upon her head a crown of twelve stars:

2 And she being with child cried, travailing in birth, and pained to be delivered.

3 And there appeared another wonder in heaven; and behold a great red dragon, having seven heads and ten horns, and seven crowns upon his heads.

4 And his tail drew the third part of the stars of heaven, and did cast them to the earth: and the dragon stood before the woman which was ready to be delivered, for to devour her child as soon as it was born.

5 And she brought forth a man child, who was to rule all nations with a rod of iron: and her child was caught up unto God, and to his throne.

6 And the woman fled into the wilderness, where she hath a place prepared of God, that they should feed her there a thousand two hundred and threescore days.

There has been much speculation among Bible prophecy experts as to precisely where this place of protection will be, and it is good to have those debates. But the truth is that we are not given the exact location, and we will just have to trust God to show us exactly where to go when the time arrives.

Most of those that hold to a pre-Trib or a mid-Trib point of view have always assumed that it would be just Jewish people that have the opportunity to flee to the wilderness during this time. And of course a lot of Jewish believers will heed the warnings of Jesus and will flee once they see the abomination of desolation. But it is my contention that there will also be a vast multitude of other believers fleeing to the mountains as well.

One place where we see a hint of this is in Revelation chapter 7. In this chapter, we are told that the 144,000 come from "all the tribes of the children of Israel"...

4 And I heard the number of them which were sealed: and there were sealed an hundred and forty and four thousand ***of all the tribes of the children of Israel.***

5 Of the tribe of Juda were sealed twelve thousand. Of the tribe of Reuben were sealed twelve thousand. Of the tribe of Gad were sealed twelve thousand.

6 Of the tribe of Aser were sealed twelve thousand. Of the tribe of Nephthalim were sealed twelve thousand. Of the tribe of Manasses were sealed twelve thousand.

7 Of the tribe of Simeon were sealed twelve thousand. Of the tribe of Levi were sealed twelve thousand. Of the tribe of Issachar were sealed twelve thousand.

8 Of the tribe of Zabulon were sealed twelve thousand. Of the tribe of Joseph were sealed twelve thousand. Of the tribe of Benjamin were sealed twelve thousand.

For centuries, many have speculated that this could not possibly be literally true.

After all, the tribe of Zebulon does not exist today.

Neither does the tribe of Asher.

Neither does Reuben.

And the list goes on and on. So how in the world can 12,000 individuals be selected out of tribes that supposedly no longer exist?

Well, before I answer that question I need to go back to the beginning.

Roughly 3000 years ago, King David and after him his son King Solomon ruled over the united kingdom of Israel. But after Solomon died, the ten northern tribes rebelled against Solomon's son Rehoboam, and from that point forward there were two kingdoms.

The ten northern tribes that rebelled against Rehoboam became known as "the house of Israel" or as "the house of Ephraim", which referred to the most dominant tribe in the northern kingdom which was Ephraim.

The three southern tribes which remained loyal to Rehoboam (Judah, Benjamin and the Levites) became known as "the house of Judah", which referred to the most dominant tribe in the southern kingdom which was Judah.

There were times when these two kingdoms were friendly, but most of the time they were not. In fact, the Jewish people (Judah) fought many very bloody wars against the northern kingdom (Israel). If you can believe it, the Bible tells us that half a million people were killed in just one of these wars (2 Chronicles 13).

Over time the people of the northern kingdom fell into great sin, and after sending prophet after prophet to warn them, God allowed them to be conquered. The northern kingdom was wiped off the face of the map by Assyria, and the remaining inhabitants of the land were exiled far from their land by the Assyrians. According to most Christian authorities, the "ten lost tribes" vanish from history at this point and will never be seen or heard from ever again.

The southern kingdom also fell into great sin, but they hung in there much longer than their northern counterparts. Eventually, Judah was conquered by Babylon, and the remaining inhabitants of the land were exiled. But as any serious student of the Bible knows, Babylon was later toppled, and the Jews returned to the land of Israel under Cyrus the king of Persia.

From that point forward, the Jewish people were almost continually dominated by one foreign power after another, and at the time when Jesus was born the foreign power that dominated the region was the Roman Empire. From time to time the Jewish people rebelled against the Romans, and eventually the Romans got fed up. In 70 AD, they destroyed Jerusalem, flattened the temple and scattered the Jewish people all throughout the known world. But even after they were scattered, the Jewish people kept their identity and their religion.

The Bible promised that in the last days the Jewish people would be regathered to the land of Israel, but for centuries prominent Christian voices proclaimed that we couldn't take those passages literally because it could never possibly happen. But God's Word is always true. The regathering of the Jewish people happened just like the Bible said that it would, and all of the doubters were silenced. It is a miracle that is unprecedented in human history, and all over the world today Bible-believing Christians rejoice in the fact that the Jewish people have been brought back home.

But that is not the end of the story. The Scriptures also tell us that the tribes of the northern kingdom will be brought back to the land and will be reunited with the southern kingdom in the last days. One place where we find this is in Ezekiel 37...

15 The word of the Lord came again unto me, saying,

16 Moreover, thou son of man, take thee one stick, and write upon it, For Judah, and for the children of Israel his companions: then take another stick, and write upon it, For Joseph, the stick of Ephraim and for all the house of Israel his companions:

17 And join them one to another into one stick; and they shall become one in thine hand.

18 And when the children of thy people shall speak unto thee, saying, Wilt thou not shew us what thou meanest by these?

19 Say unto them, **Thus saith the Lord God; Behold, I will take the stick of Joseph, which is in the hand of Ephraim, and the tribes of Israel his fellows, and will put them with him, even with the stick of Judah, and make them one stick, and they shall be one in mine hand.**

20 And the sticks whereon thou writest shall be in thine hand before their eyes.

21 And say unto them, Thus saith the Lord God; Behold, I will take the children of Israel from among the heathen, whither they be gone, and will gather them on every side, and bring them into their own land:

22 And I will make them one nation in the land upon the mountains of Israel; and one king shall be king to them all: and they shall be no more two nations, neither shall they be divided into two kingdoms any more at all.

Once again, most prominent Christian voices are saying that this is absolutely impossible and that we should not take these promises literally. The descendants of the northern kingdom have lost their identity and they don't even know who they are anymore. In addition, the land where they once lived is one of the most hotly contested pieces of real estate on the entire planet. Virtually every other country in the world wants to give the region known as "Samaria" to the Palestinians as part of their new state.

But as we have seen so many times before, the Word of God is always true in the end. Revelation chapter 7 says that the tribes of the northern kingdom will exist as distinct entities in the last days, and they will be regathered to the land just like the Bible says.

In Hosea chapter 1, we are told that the children of the northern kingdom "shall be as the sand of the sea" even after they are exiled. And we are also told that someday the exiled descendants of the House of Israel will be reunited with Judah, and they will live exactly where they lived before. In fact, Hosea says that in the exact place where it was said that they were not God's people, there they will be called "the sons of the living God"...

*10 Yet the number of the children of Israel shall be as the sand of the sea, which cannot be measured nor numbered; and it shall come to pass, that **in the place where it was said unto them, Ye are not my people, there it shall be said unto them, Ye are the sons of the living God**.*

*11 **Then shall the children of Judah and the children of Israel be gathered together**, and appoint themselves one head, and they shall come up out of the land: for great shall be the day of Jezreel.*

For much, much more on this, please see Isaiah chapter 11, Jeremiah chapters 23, 30 and 31, Zechariah 10, Ezekiel 36 and 37, and the end of the first three chapters of Hosea. And for a two hour presentation on the historical migrations of the people descended from the "ten lost tribes", please see my DVD entitled "The Regathering of the Ten Lost Tribes of Israel".

The truth is that we know a whole lot about where the people of the northern kingdom migrated, and they truly did become "as the sand of the sea" just like the book of Hosea said they would. And just like Hosea, Ezekiel and other Old Testament prophets foresaw, they will be gathered back to the land of Israel in the last days.

But the truth is that it does not matter what your DNA is. Just like the first exodus out of Egypt, the coming regathering back to the land of Israel will be made up of a "mixed multitude". As the persecution of Christians greatly intensifies in future years, vast numbers of believers will be looking for somewhere safe to go, and I am convinced that the land of Israel will become the number one destination.

At that time, perhaps Satan will think that he has gathered the Christians and Jews together for one final slaughter, but

God has something else in mind. I believe that the land of Israel will be ground zero for the greatest move of God the world has ever seen, and as I discussed at the beginning of this chapter, there will be a place of protection available for the Remnant once the time of the abomination of desolation comes.

I know that I have covered an enormous amount of material very rapidly in this chapter. The truth is that I could fill an entire college course on just this topic alone. In the end, I want you to understand that there will be somewhere that you and your family can go during the challenging days to come. God will provide a place of protection for the Remnant, but if people hold on to their pre-Trib or mid-Trib rapture theories too tightly, they might end up totally missing out on God's plan.

-CHAPTER THIRTY FIVE-

Jesus Is Coming Soon

Where would you rather be than right here, right now?

For my wife and I, there is no other time in human history that we would have rather been alive for. We have reached the culmination of all things. The King is coming! We truly are living in Biblical times, and we are fully convinced that the greatest chapters of our lives are still ahead of us.

I know that I have shared some very hard things in this book, and I really wanted to wrap things up on a positive note. Because as immensely challenging as the days ahead will be, the truth is that the trials that we will face are nothing compared to the glory that is about to be revealed. Our Lord and Savior, Jesus Christ, is coming back and we will never be separated from Him again.

And as I mentioned in previous chapters, in the time between right now and when Jesus does return, I believe that we are going to see the greatest move of God the world has ever known and the greatest harvest of souls in all of church history.

Who wouldn't want to be right in the middle of that?

So in the midst of all the talk about tribulation and judgments and persecution, let us not forget the bigger picture. The population of the world is larger today than it has ever been throughout all of human history, and so there is more of an opportunity to bring people into the kingdom than ever before.

Once Jesus comes back, the time for evangelism will be over. But right now, the fate of billions of souls hangs in the balance, and it is up to us to get the job done.

Yes, our lives are about to change. Everything that can be shaken will be shaken, and those that are living for worldly things will plunge into depression and despair.

But of course as believers our lives are not supposed to be about the things of this world anyway. Everything that we see around us is passing away, and this is not our home. Instead, we look forward to something far better. I love how the Apostle Paul put it in Romans 8:18...

For I reckon that the sufferings of this present time **are not worthy to be compared** *with the glory which shall be revealed in us.*

I believe that many of us are actually going to get to see with our very eyes what Christians have been eagerly anticipating for nearly two thousand years – the triumphant return of Jesus Christ to this planet.

And in the short time that we have left, we are going to experience the finest hour in the history of the church. We are going to see things happen that most of us would not even dare to imagine right now.

For me, it is hard to put into words the great opportunity that is ahead of us. We have the chance to be the generation that finally gets things right, and we have been given the task of preparing the way for the return of the Lord.

I don't know about you, but my wife and I desperately want to participate in the great harvest of souls that is coming. We constantly pray that God would allow us to be on the cutting edge of what He is doing in these last days, but there is no guarantee that any of us are going to get to be part of it. It is those that have their hearts right with God and that are seeking Him with all that they have that He is going to use.

The debt-fueled standard of living that we are all enjoying right now is about to disappear. This is something that I have written more than a million words about on *The Economic Collapse Blog*. We are entering a time of great social chaos, nightmarish natural disasters and unprecedented global war.

But when times are the darkest, that is when the greatest heroes are needed.

Just think about it. If you look back throughout history, what do the great leaders that we admire the most have in common?

Most of them arose during times of great crisis. Despite great challenges, they stood strong and chose to make a difference.

It is when times are the darkest that light is needed the most. You were born for such a time as this, and God is calling us to rise and shine in this dark hour.

We live in a world that is literally starving for meaning and purpose. And most people in the western world today have little meaning and purpose to their lives other than going to work, paying the bills and trying to make it through another day.

But as Christians, our outlook is entirely different. We have read the end of the book, and we know that the ultimate happy ending is ahead of us. And every day we have a chance to make an impact for eternity. What could be better than helping even a single person find eternal life through Jesus Christ?

We are building the kingdom of our Lord and Savior, and we are engaged in constant warfare with the kingdom of darkness. Clothed in the armor of God, we fight on even in the midst of overwhelming challenges. We are called children of the Most High, and we are destined for greatness. God has taken the broken pieces of our lives and has turned them into a beautiful thing. We love Him because He first loved us, and we would lay down our lives for Him without a moment's hesitation.

Without God we can do nothing, but with Him all things are possible.

In the days ahead, a lot of people are going to try to hide from all of the trouble that is happening. But that is not what we are called to do. We are called to run to the battle. We are called to be radically sold out warriors for our Lord and Savior. We are called to rescue as many souls from the kingdom of darkness as we can while there is still time. The Word of God tells us that the gates of hell will not prevail against us. We are more than conquerors, and we will overcome the enemy by the Blood of the Lamb and by the word of our testimony.

Can you hear the dry bones shake? The remnant of the living God is rising up in power. There has never been a time like this in human history, and there will never be a time like it ever again. We are going to write the final chapters of the history of the church, and this is going to be our finest hour.

The closer we get to the "parousia", the worse the persecution of Christians is going to become. By the time it is all said and done, millions upon millions of us are going to be struck down for our faith. But we will never back down. We will be faithful even unto death, and in the end we shall receive a crown of life.

Through it all, we are going to become the people that God created us to be, and we are going to learn to truly love one another. While the world is coming apart at the seams all around us, the Remnant is going to pull together and work in unity. We can change the world – if we will just believe.

No matter what the obstacle, no matter what the challenge, and no matter what the odds look like, we will press forward. And whether we live or die, we can look forward to that day when the final trumpet will sound and we will be taken home.

As I write this, I am reminded of the last verse of one of my favorite hymns...

And, Lord, haste the day when my faith shall be sight,

the clouds be rolled back as a scroll;

the trump shall resound, and the Lord shall descend,

even so, it is well with my soul.

Come quickly Lord Jesus. We love you and we can't wait to see you. And while we remain here, we will endeavor to win as many precious souls for the kingdom as we can while there is still time. Amen.

-CHAPTER THIRTY SIX-

101 Key Points To Remember

1. The "rapture" and "the resurrection" are two different terms that describe the exact same event. (1 Thessalonians 4, 1 Corinthians 15)

2. Revelation 20 tells us that the "first resurrection" comes immediately after the Tribulation is over. (Revelation 20)

3. In Revelation chapter 20, we are told that the "first resurrection" includes those that do not worship the beast or his image and that do not receive his mark on their foreheads or their hands.

4. There is a very important Greek word that shows up in rapture passages throughout the New Testament. That word is "parousia", and it can be translated "coming", "arrival", "presence" or "official visit".

5. Multiple passages tell us that the rapture will happen at the "coming" ("parousia") of Christ, and the New Testament also makes it clear that this "coming" ("parousia") will come immediately after the end of the seven year Tribulation period. (1 Thessalonians 4, 1 Corinthians 15, Matthew 24, 2 Thessalonians 2)

6. In Matthew 24, Jesus tells us that the rapture will happen "immediately after the Tribulation". Similar passages can be found in Mark 13 and Luke 21.

7. In Matthew 24, 1 Thessalonians 4 and Revelation 14 we are told that Jesus comes in the clouds in all three passages. That is because all three passages are describing the exact same event.

8. In Matthew 24, 1 Thessalonians 4 and 1 Corinthians 15 we are told that a great trumpet is blown when believers are raptured. That is because all three passages are describing the exact same event.

9. In 1 Corinthians 15, we are specifically told that the rapture will happen at "the last trumpet".

10. In Matthew 24, 1 Thessalonians 4 and 1 Corinthians 15 the exact same Greek word for trumpet ("salpigx") is used in all three instances.

11. The trumpet blasts of Matthew 24, 1 Thessalonians 4 and 1 Corinthians 15 all correspond to the blowing of the 7th trumpet in the book of Revelation.

12. When the last trumpet is blown in Revelation 11, we are told that it is "the time of the dead, that they should be judged" and that it is the time when Jesus will reward those that belong to Him. We are also told that this is the time when our Messiah begins to reign.

13. The seven year Tribulation period is also known as "Daniel's 70th week" and "the Time of Jacob's Trouble", and it comes to an end when the 7th trumpet is blown. (Revelation 11)

14. Once the 7th trumpet is blown, the rapture takes place, and it begins a period of time known as "the Millennial reign", "the last day" and "the Day of the Lord". (Revelation 11)

15. In Revelation chapter 14, we find the rapture exactly where it should be in the chronology of the last days. We find it described after the seventh trumpet is sounded but before the first of the vial judgments is poured out.

16. The Biblical feast days that take place in the fall provide a template for the events that immediately follow the Tribulation. Just as the spring feasts were "dress rehearsals" for the crucifixion, death, burial and resurrection of our Savior, so the fall feasts are also prophetically foreshadowing precisely what will happen during His second coming.

17. The "last trumpet" will be blown on Rosh Hashanah (the Feast of Trumpets) on the day after the end of the Tribulation period during some future year.

18. Immediately following the rapture, in Revelation chapter 15 we see a great group of believers gathered around the throne of God giving Him praise. This group of believers includes those "that had gotten the victory over the beast, and over his image, and over his mark, and over the number of his name". It is very interesting to note that from this point forward there are no more mentions of believers on the earth until we return with Jesus in Revelation chapter 19.

19. In Revelation chapter 16, the seven vials of God's wrath are poured out. These judgments come in rapid fire succession, and none of them require an extended period of time.

20. The vial judgments are poured out during "the Days of Awe" that stretch from Rosh Hashanah (the Feast of Trumpets) to when we victoriously return with our Lord and Savior to set up His kingdom on Yom Kippur (the Day of Atonement).

21. In Revelation 19, we find the marriage of the Lamb just where we would expect it to be. It comes after the rapture in Revelation 14 but before the return of Jesus for the Battle of Armageddon later on in Revelation 19.

22. The victorious return of Jesus Christ with His army on Yom Kippur is described in vivid detail in Revelation 19, Joel 2 and other places throughout Scripture.

23. If you look at Matthew 24:29 in many versions of the Bible, you will notice that there is a little footnote pointing you to Joel 2:10. Joel chapter 2 is an extended description of the coming of the Day of the Lord, and in Matthew 24 Jesus is indicating that this is the exact period of time during which the rapture will take place. It is important to remember that while the rapture and the return of Jesus with His army are very close together, they do not both happen within the same 24 hour time period. The rapture is on Rosh Hashanah, and we return with the Lord on Yom Kippur.

24. In the end, the Antichrist will be totally defeated, and the Lord Jesus Christ will reign from Jerusalem over the whole planet for 1000 years. (Revelation 20)

25. There is not a single verse in the Bible that tells us that Christians will be raptured before the Tribulation.

26. There is not a single verse in the Bible that tells us that Christians will be raptured in the middle of the Tribulation.

27. The church is going to go through the entire Tribulation period. (Matthew 24, Mark 13, Revelation 14, Revelation 20)

28. In 1 Thessalonians 5, the Apostle Paul links the timing of the rapture with the coming of the Day of the Lord. In that passage, Paul says that the Day of the Lord comes "as a thief in the night".

29. In 2 Peter 3, the Apostle Peter also tells us that the Day of the Lord comes "as a thief in the night".

30. Zechariah 14 describes the coming of the Day of the Lord, and it specifically mentions that it will be at this time that Jesus will once again set foot on the Mount of Olives.

31. Joel 2 also describes the coming of the Day of the Lord. In that chapter, we are told that at that time the Lord will personally lead the greatest army in the history of the world back to Jerusalem.

32. In Matthew 24, Jesus makes reference to Joel 2 while He is speaking about the timing of the rapture.

33. Isaiah 13 also speaks about the coming of the Day of the Lord, and it also has language that very closely parallels Matthew 24.

34. Daniel 9:27 tells us that the abomination of desolation happens in the middle of the Tribulation, and in Matthew 24 Jesus tells us that the rapture comes after that event.

35. In Matthew 24, we are also told that the abomination of desolation starts a period of persecution unlike anything the world has ever seen before. Believers in Israel are instructed to flee to the mountains where there will be a place of protection.

36. Revelation 12 and other passages tell us that believers in this place of protection will be kept safe for a period of approximately three and a half years.

37. Immediately after the tribulation ("thlipsis") of those days the rapture will take place.

38. On Rosh Hashanah, traditionally there is a series of 100 shofar blasts. The very last of these trumpet blasts is known as the "Tekiah Gedolah" or "the last trumpet".

39. At the blowing of the last trumpet in Revelation 11, we are told that the time has come for the dead to be judged.

40. At the blowing of the last trumpet in Revelation 11, we are told that the time has come for Jesus to begin His reign. This marks the beginning of "the Day of the Lord" also known as "the last day" and the Millennial reign.

41. In John 6, Jesus tells us four times that those that believe in Him will be resurrected "at the last day".

42. In Revelation 14, we see one described as "the Son of Man" with a golden crown on his head coming on the clouds and harvesting the earth.

43. The same Greek word ("nephele") that is used to identify clouds in Matthew 24 and 1 Thessalonians 4 is also used in Revelation 14.

44. In Revelation 15, we find the vast multitude of believers that were raptured in Revelation 14 standing before the throne of God giving him praise. This group of believers includes those "that had gotten the victory over the beast, and over his image, and over his mark, and over the number of his name".

45. In 2 Thessalonians 2, we are given specific signs that must happen before the rapture takes place. One of those signs is the revealing of the Antichrist.

46. 2 Thessalonians 2 also tells us that we will know who the Antichrist is when he goes into the temple of God and proclaims himself to be God. This is a reference to the abomination of desolation which comes in the middle of the Tribulation.

47. In Revelation 13, we are told that the Antichrist conducts a war against the saints. How is that possible if all of the saints had already been raptured?

48. In Revelation 13, we are told that the war against the saints lasts for 42 months. This breaks down to about three and a half years.

49. In Daniel 7, we are also told that the war against the saints will last for approximately three and a half years.

50. In Matthew 24, we learn that the war against the saints begins in the middle of the Tribulation, and that we are raptured immediately after those days are over.

51. In an attempt to square their theology with what the Bible actually says, the pre-Trib crowd has come up with the concept of "Tribulation saints". But nowhere in the Bible is the term "Tribulation saints" ever used, and there is no mention of masses of people getting saved after a rapture event. This is a doctrine that theologians have made up out of thin air.

52. If there was going to be a pre-Tribulation rapture, you would expect to find the marriage of the Lamb near the very beginning of the book of Revelation. Instead, you find it in Revelation 19.

53. Every one of the festivals of the Lord represented a "dress rehearsal" for future events. The spring feasts are a prophetic template that foreshadowed the major events of the first coming of Jesus, and the fall feasts are a prophetic template that foreshadow the major events of the second coming of Jesus.

54. The Feast of Trumpets ("Rosh Hashanah") has also been known since ancient times as "the Hidden Feast". The reason

it is called this is because in ancient times nobody ever quite knew when it was going to begin. The Feast of Trumpets falls on the first day of the seventh month on the Hebrew calendar, but the new month could not begin until the new moon was spotted. Once the new moon was finally spotted, then the Feast of Trumpets could officially commence. That is why even today the Jewish people allocate two days for the celebration of this festival.

55. The phrase "no man knows the day or the hour" was commonly used to refer to the Feast of Trumpets in ancient Israel. So when Jesus used this phrase, He was pointing us to this holiday.

56. The Day of Atonement ("Yom Kippur") will be the day when Jesus returns with His army, defeats the forces of the Antichrist, and sets down on the Mount of Olives.

57. Passages in the book of Joel that call for fasting and a solemn assembly are keys that help us connect the physical return of Jesus to this planet to the festival of Yom Kippur.

58. In Revelation 19, we see Jesus wearing a robe dipped in blood and the army of heaven wearing white. These are other key details that link the festival of Yom Kippur to these prophetic events.

59. The final fall festival, the Feast of Tabernacles, is a time of great rejoicing. The theme of the festival can be described as "God dwelling with man", and many believe that it will be the time when Jesus takes His place on the throne in Jerusalem (Ezekiel 43) to rule over this world for a thousand years (Revelation 20). In fact, Zechariah 14 specifically mentions the fact that Jesus will require the whole world to celebrate the Feast of Tabernacles once He returns.

60. When the Bible tells us that we are not appointed to wrath, it is not telling us that we are going to get pulled out of here before the Tribulation begins. It is simply telling us that because we have been saved through faith in Jesus Christ we are not destined for hell. (1 Thessalonians 5:9-10)

61. In John 16:33, Jesus promises us that we "shall have tribulation" while we are in this world.

62. In 1 Peter 4, we are instructed to "think it not strange" when we have to endure fiery trials.

63. In Acts 14, we are told "that we must through much tribulation enter into the kingdom of God".

64. In Matthew 24, Matthew 25 and Mark 13, Jesus told His disciples that no man knows the day or the hour of His coming. In all of those instances, the only "coming" that was discussed in those conversations was the coming of Jesus immediately after the Tribulation. It is impossible for those verses to be referring to a pre-Tribulation rapture, because in each instance Jesus had just told His disciples that He is coming after the Tribulation.

65. It is also important to note that in Matthew 24, Matthew 25 and Mark 13, Jesus was speaking in the present tense when He stated that no man knows the day or the hour. We cannot take a statement made in the present tense and apply it indefinitely.

66. Rosh Hashanah (the Feast of Trumpets) was always called the "day and hour which no man knows" in ancient Israel. The reason for this is the fact that Rosh Hashanah always falls on the first day of the seventh month, and the holiday could not be officially declared until the new moon

was spotted. In ancient Israel, the authorities were never quite sure when that would be.

67. In 1 Thessalonians 5, we are told that the Day of the Lord comes as a "thief in the night", and in verse 4 we are also specifically told that since we are believers that this day should not overtake us as a thief.

68. If Jesus comes as a "thief in the night" before the Tribulation, then why does He say "I come as a thief" in Revelation 16:15 at the end of the Tribulation?

69. In 2 Thessalonians 2, the identity of "the Restrainer" is never revealed. But even if the Restrainer is the Holy Spirit, it is not at all necessary for the Holy Spirit to be totally removed from our planet for Him to stop restraining the Antichrist. In fact, we find the Holy Spirit very active in the book of Revelation long after the Antichrist has been revealed.

70. It is exceedingly important to remember that the passage about "the Restrainer" in 2 Thessalonians 2 comes immediately after verses where the Apostle Paul specifically warns us that the rapture will not occur until after the Antichrist is revealed and the abomination of desolation takes place.

71. Titus 2 tells us about "the blessed hope", but nowhere in that passage does it say anything about a pre-Tribulation rapture. To equate "the blessed hope" with a pre-Tribulation rapture is simply not consistent with Scripture.

72. In 2 Timothy 3, the Apostle Paul warns us that all who seek to live godly lives in Christ Jesus will suffer persecution.

73. In 1 Thessalonians 3, Paul specifically tells us that we are appointed to persecution.

74. In Revelation 4, the Apostle John is told to "come up hither". Pre-Trib advocates say that this is a picture of the rapture, but that is just an attempt to read something into Scripture that simply is not there. And such an interpretation would directly contradict the rest of the book of Revelation and the remainder of the Bible.

75. The word "church" is never used after Revelation 4, but numerous references are made to believers living on the earth all throughout the book of Revelation (Revelation 7:3-8; 11:3-6; 12:11; 12:17; 13:7-10; 14:12).

76. In Revelation 7, we see a great multitude around the throne of God that had just come "out of the great tribulation". Pre-Trib advocates imagine that these are believers that were raptured before the Tribulation began. But in order to "come out" of something, you have to already be in it, and this gathering does not happen until the sixth seal. In addition, there are no indications in the surrounding context of a "rapture" or a "resurrection" taking place. The most logical explanation is that these are believers that were among the hundreds of millions of people that died during the preceding seal judgments. Such an explanation is consistent with Revelation 11, Revelation 14, Revelation 20 and the rest of the rapture passages that we find all throughout the Bible.

77. In Revelation 6, we see the sun being darkened and the moon becoming as blood. Many want to tie this passage to a similar passage in Matthew 24, and at first glance that seems to make sense. But upon closer examination we see that there are fundamental differences between Revelation 6 and Matthew 24. One example is that the moon gives no light at all in Matthew 24, but in Revelation 6 the moon becomes "as

blood" meaning that it appears to be red. But in order for the moon to be red, light must be coming from the moon.

78. There is a perfect match between Matthew 24, Joel 2 and Isaiah 13. All three instances speak of the sun being darkened and the moon giving no light. And all three instances point to the coming of the Day of the Lord at the end of the Tribulation period.

79. The doctrine of the pre-Tribulation rapture was popularized by some extremely questionable people less than 200 years ago. Before Margaret MacDonald, the Irvingites and John Darby came along, the dominant position all throughout church history was that the resurrection would happen at the return of Jesus at the end of the Tribulation period.

80. Four separate times in John 6, Jesus explains that those who follow Him will be raised up "at the last day".

81. In 2 Peter 3:8, we are told that the Lord considers "a thousand years as one day".

82. Genesis 6:3 seems to indicate that the Lord will strive with man for 120 jubilee cycles, which would work out to precisely 6000 years.

83. 2 Peter 3, Joel 2, Isaiah 13 and other passages tell us that the coming of the Day of the Lord (the 7th thousand years) will be a time of great turmoil. This is precisely what we see in the book of Revelation.

84. According to ancient Jewish tradition, Rosh Hashanah (the Feast of Trumpets) is "the birthday of the world". I am convinced that this marked the beginning of the "first day", and it is when God's prophetic clock started. Moving forward 6000 years from that date, it brings us to another

Rosh Hashanah, which is exactly when I believe the rapture will take place. And I am also convinced that the seven year Tribulation period will also start on a Rosh Hashanah exactly seven years earlier.

85. In Revelation 11, we see the announcement of the beginning of "the 7th day" of human history. At this point the 7 year Tribulation ends, and the Millennial reign (also known as "the Day of the Lord" and "the last day") begins.

86. In Daniel 12, we are also told that the resurrection of believers immediately follows a period of great tribulation.

87. In both 1 Thessalonians 4 and Daniel 12, we see the archangel Michael discussed in conjunction with the rapture.

88. In both Daniel 12 and Matthew 24, the abomination of desolation starts off a period of great tribulation unlike anything the world has ever seen before. Daniel tells us that this period of time will last for approximately three and a half years, and both Daniel and Matthew tell us that the rapture of God's people will take place immediately after the time of tribulation is over.

89. Revelation 1:7 refers to the second coming of Jesus, and we are told that "every eye shall see him".

90. Other passages that completely rule out a "secret rapture" include 2 Peter 3:10, Luke 17 and Matthew 24.

91. When Christians start realizing that there is not going to be a pre-Tribulation rapture, many of them will become extremely upset with the preachers that had been promising them one.

92. When global events start spinning out of control and everyone starts saying that the Tribulation is here, the

mocking of those that believe in a pre-Tribulation rapture is going to reach epic proportions. (2 Peter 3:3-4)

93. Any Christian leader that chooses to teach about the events of the last days and the timing of the rapture is taking on a great deal of responsibility. If you are one of these leaders, you should know that people are making decisions on whether or not to get prepared based on what you are telling them.

94. As it stands, there are millions upon millions of believers that are utterly unprepared physically, mentally, emotionally and spiritually for what is ahead.

95. As global events spiral out of control over the next few years, it is going to become very popular to say that we have already entered the seven year Tribulation period. But the truth, of course, is that the Tribulation has not started yet, nor are we about to enter that period of time.

96. There are still certain things that must happen before the Tribulation begins. One of them is the rise of the ten-horned one world government that is described in the book of Daniel and the book of Revelation.

97. Another thing that we are watching for is the rebuilding of the Jewish temple in Jerusalem. This has to be completed by the midpoint of the Tribulation period so that the Antichrist can commit the "abomination of desolation" mentioned in Matthew 24.

98. The judgment of God on America is imminent. I believe that 2015 was a year when America was pronounced guilty. Now the judgment of God is coming, and we are going to deserve every ounce of what is about to happen to us.

99. God is raising up a Remnant that will keep His commandments, that will bring in the greatest harvest of souls the world has ever seen, and that will move in the power of the Holy Spirit in ways that we have not seen since the first century. God is in the process of restoring all things, and we are going to be the generation that finally gets things right. The greatest move of God of all time is going to happen right before the return of our Lord and Savior Jesus Christ, and we are going to become the kind of bride that He deserves. On our own, this is impossible, but with Him all things are possible.

100. God has a plan, and there is going to be somewhere for the Remnant to go. This place of protection is mentioned in Matthew 24 and numerous other passages.

101. Jesus is coming back soon, there is a great deal of work to be done, and the fate of billions of souls hangs in the balance.

-CHAPTER THIRTY SEVEN-

The Most Important Thing

When Jesus comes back to gather His people, will you be one of them? Perhaps you have been reading this book and you have been thinking that you are not sure if you belong to Jesus or not. The good news is that you can know for certain where you will spend eternity, and God wants you to be part of His family.

Yes, the years immediately ahead of us are going to be extremely challenging. And if you are a Christian, you will likely face great persecution.

But things are going to be even harder for those that do not know Jesus. Personally, I have no idea how anyone is going to make it through what is coming without a strong relationship with God. I know that I wouldn't want to face the years ahead without Him.

And it is a fact that this life does not go on indefinitely. There are some people that get insurance policies for just about anything and everything, but they don't even give a second thought to what will happen to them once they die.

At the end of every book that I write, I like to include a section on the most important thing that I could possibly talk about. If I had not given my life to the Lord Jesus Christ, I would probably be dead today. He has taken the broken pieces of my life and has turned them into a beautiful thing, and He can do the same thing for you.

If you would like to know how you can become a Christian, I encourage you to keep reading. A lot of the time people find Christianity to be very confusing. In the following pages, I have tried to explain the core of the Christian faith in a way that hopefully just about everyone will be able to understand.

Fortunately, the Christian gospel is very, very simple to understand, and the stakes are incredibly high.

If Christianity is true, then it is possible to have eternal life.

I am not just talking about living for millions of years or billions of years.

I am talking about living for eternity.

If you had the opportunity to live forever, would you take it?

Many people would respond by saying that they are not sure if living forever in a world like ours would be desirable, but what if you could live forever in a world where everything had been set right?

What if you could live forever in a perfect world where there is no more evil or suffering or pain?

Would you want that?

The truth is that this is exactly what God wants for you. He loves you very much and He wants to spend forever with you.

If you could, would you want to spend forever with Him?

If God is real, and there really is an afterlife, who wouldn't want to spend eternity with Him?

To be honest with you, if eternal life really exists, there is not a single issue of greater importance to every man, woman and child on the planet.

Who would not be willing to give up everything that they own to live forever in paradise surrounded by people that love them?

All over the world people perform all kinds of religious acts, desperately hoping that they will gain favor with God. Some religious nuts even blow themselves up during suicide attacks, hoping that their "sacrifices" will earn them favor with God. But are those really ways to get to heaven?

Of course not.

God did not make it complicated to reach out to Him. The truth is that the plan of salvation described in the Bible is very simple.

It starts with God.

The Bible tells us that God created humanity and that He loves us very much.

In fact, God loves you more than you could possibly ever imagine. The Scriptures go on and on about how great the love of God is and about how deeply He cares for each one of us individually.

But there is a huge problem.

The problem is that humanity is in deep rebellion against God.

Humanity has rejected God and is continually breaking His laws.

Most people like to think of themselves as "good" people, but the truth is that none of us are truly "good". Each one of us has broken God's laws over and over again. We are lawbreakers and criminals in the sight of God. The Scriptures call us sinners.

Perhaps you think that you are a "good person" and that God should let you into heaven based on how good you are.

If that is what you believe, ask yourself this question...

Have you ever broken God's laws?

Posted below is a summary of the Ten Commandments. Are you guilty of violating His ways?...

#1) You shall have no other gods before Me. (There is only one true God – the Creator of all things. Have you ever served a different God? Have you ever expressed approval for a false religion just because you wanted to be polite? Have you ever participated in activities or ceremonies that honor other religions?)

#2) You shall not make any idols. You shall not bow down to them or serve them. (The Scriptures tell us that we are to love God with everything that we have inside of us. Even if you have never bowed down to an idol or a statue, you may have created a "god" in your own mind that you are more comfortable with. That is sin. In fact, we are not to have any "idols" in our lives that we love more than God.)

#3) You shall not take the name of the Lord your God in vain. (Have you ever used God's holy name as a profanity or as a curse word? Have you ever failed to give His holy name the honor that it deserves?)

#4) Remember the Sabbath Day, to keep it holy. (Is there anyone alive that has kept this commandment perfectly?)

#5) Honor your father and mother. (Have you ever been rebellious or disrespectful to your father or your mother even one time? If so, you have broken this commandment.)

#6) You shall not murder. (Even if you have never killed anyone, it is important to remember that Jesus considers hatred to be very similar to murder.)

#7) You shall not commit adultery. (Sexual promiscuity is absolutely rampant in our society today, but you don't even have to sleep with someone to break this commandment. In Matthew 5:27-28, Jesus said that "whosoever looketh on a woman to lust after her hath committed adultery with her already in his heart".)

#8) You shall not steal. (Have you ever stolen anything from someone else? It doesn't matter if it was valuable or not. If you stole something, you are a thief.)

#9) You shall not lie. (Have you ever told a lie? If so, you are guilty of breaking this commandment.)

#10) You shall not covet. (Have you ever jealously desired something that belongs to someone else? This sin is often the first step toward other sins.)

The first four commandments are about loving God. In the Scriptures, you are commanded to love God with all of your heart, all of your soul, all of your mind and all of your strength.

The final six commandments are about loving others. In the Scriptures, you are commanded to love others as you love yourself.

Have you always loved God and loved others like you should have?

Sadly, the truth is that we are all guilty of breaking God's laws.

In fact, if we took an honest look at how guilty we truly are we would be absolutely horrified.

Take a moment and imagine the following scenario...

One of the biggest television networks has decided to do a huge two hour prime time special all about your life. It is going to be heavily advertised, and tens of millions of people are going to watch it.

Doesn't that sound great?

But instead of a two hour documentary about how wonderful you are, the network has discovered all of the most evil and horrible things that you have ever thought, said or did and they are going to broadcast those things to tens of millions of people all over the world for two hours during prime time.

What would you do if that happened?

Sadly, the truth is that whoever that happened to would be utterly ashamed and would never want to be seen in public again.

Why?

Because we have all done, said and thought things that are unspeakably evil.

We are sinners in the eyes of God, just as the Scriptures tell us...

"For all have sinned, and come short of the glory of God" (Romans 3:23)

God created us to have fellowship with Him, but He also gave humanity the ability to choose. Unfortunately, humanity has chosen to be in deep rebellion against God and we have all repeatedly broken His laws. When we broke God's commandments, our fellowship with God was also broken. By breaking God's commandments, we decided that our will would be done instead of God's will. And if you look around the world today, you can see the results. Evil and suffering are everywhere. God hates all of this evil and suffering very much. In the Bible, our rebellion against God is called sin.

As a result of our sin, the Scriptures tell us that we are separated from God...

"The wages of sin is death" [spiritual separation from God] (Romans 6:23)

So what can be done about this separation from God?

Why doesn't God just forget about our sins?

Well, the truth is that God cannot just sweep our evil under the rug. If God did that, He would cease to be just.

For example, how would you feel about a judge that decided to issue a blanket pardon for Hitler and all of the other high level Nazis for the horrible things that they did?

Would that be a "good" judge? Of course not.

There is a penalty for evil, and because God is just, that penalty must be paid.

Fortunately, Jesus Christ paid the penalty for our sins by dying for us on the cross. He took the punishment that we deserved...

"But God commendeth his love toward us, in that, while we were yet sinners, Christ died for us." (Romans 5:8)

We were guilty, but the Son of God, Jesus Christ, died in our place.

Being fully man, Jesus could die for the sins of mankind.

Being fully God, Jesus could die for an infinite number of sins.

He was mocked, He was beaten, He was scourged ruthlessly and He was nailed to a wooden cross. He was totally innocent, but He was willing to suffer and die because He loved you that much.

Jesus paid the penalty for your sins and my sins so that fellowship with God could be restored.

Not only that, but Jesus proved that He is the Son of God by rising from the dead...

"Christ died for our sins...He was buried...He rose again the third day according to the Scriptures" (1 Corinthians 15:3-4)

You see, if there was any other way for us to be reconciled to God, Jesus would not have had to die on the cross. He could have just told us to follow one of the other ways to get to heaven. But there was no other way. The death of Jesus on the cross is the only payment for our sins and He is the only way that we are going to get to heaven. In the Scriptures, Jesus put it this way...

"I am the way, the truth, and the life: no man cometh unto the Father, but by me." (John 14:6)

But it is not enough just for you to intellectually know that Jesus is the Son of God and that He died on the cross for our sins.

The Scriptures tell us that we must individually commit our lives to Jesus Christ as Savior and Lord. When we give our lives to Jesus, He forgives our sins and He gives us eternal life...

"But as many as received him, to them gave he power to become the sons of God, even to them that believe on his name" (John 1:12)

"For God so loved the world, that he gave his only begotten Son, that whosoever believeth in him should not perish, but have everlasting life." (John 3:16)

"That if thou shalt confess with thy mouth the Lord Jesus, and shalt believe in thine heart that God hath raised him from the dead, thou shalt be saved." (Romans 10:9)

So exactly how does someone do this?

It is actually very simple.

The Scriptures tell us that it is through faith that we enter into a relationship with Jesus Christ...

"For by grace are ye saved through faith; and that not of yourselves: it is the gift of God: Not of works, lest any man should boast." (Ephesians 2:8,9)

If you are not a Christian yet, then Jesus is standing at the door of your heart and He is knocking. He is hoping that you will let Him come in. He loves you very much and He wants to have a relationship with you...

[Jesus speaking] "Behold, I stand at the door, and knock: if any man hear my voice, and open the door, I will come in to him" (Revelation 3:20)

Jesus asks that you give Him complete control of your life. That means renouncing all of the sin in your life and making Him your Savior and Lord. Just to know intellectually that Jesus died on the cross and that He rose from the dead is not enough to become a Christian. Having a wonderful emotional experience is not enough to become a Christian either. You become a Christian by faith. It is an act of your will.

Are you ready to make a commitment to Jesus Christ?

If you are ready to invite Jesus Christ into your life, it is very easy.

Just tell Him.

God is not really concerned if you say the right words. What He is concerned about is the attitude of your heart.

If you are ready to become a Christian, the following is a prayer that can help you express that desire to Him...

"Lord Jesus, I want to become a Christian. I know that I am a sinner, and I thank you for dying on the cross for my sins. I believe that you are the Son of God and that you rose from the dead. I repent of my sins and I open the door of my life and ask you to be my Savior and Lord. I commit my life to you. Thank you for forgiving all of my sins and giving me eternal life. Take control of my life and make me the kind of person that you want me to be. I will live my life for you. Amen."

If you are ready to enter into a personal relationship with Jesus Christ, then I invite you to pray this prayer right now. Jesus will come into your life, just as He has promised that He would.

If you just invited Jesus Christ to come into your life, you can have 100 percent certainty that you have become a Christian and that you will go to heaven when you die. In 1 John 5:11-13, the Scriptures tell us the following...

"And this is the record, that God hath given to us eternal life, and this life is in his Son. He that hath the Son hath life; and he that hath not the Son of God hath not life. These things have I written unto you that believe on the name of the Son of God; that ye may know that ye have eternal life".

Do you understand what that means?

It means that you can know that you have eternal life.

The Bible says that if you have invited Jesus Christ into your life, your sins are forgiven and you now have eternal life.

What could be better than that?

But your journey is not done.

In fact, it is just beginning.

The Christian life is not easy - especially if you try to go it alone.

There are four keys to spiritual growth for any Christian...

#1) The Bible - If you do not have a Bible you will need to get one and read it every day. It is God's instruction book for your life.

#2) Prayer – Prayer does not have to be complicated. The truth is that prayer is just talking with God. God wants to hear from you every day, and He will fundamentally transform your life as you pray to Him with humility and sincerity.

#3) Fellowship - The Scriptures tell us that we all need each other. Find a fellowship of local Christians that believe the Bible and that sincerely love one another. They will help you grow.

#4) Witnessing - Tell others about the new life that you have found in Jesus Christ. Helping even one person find eternal life is of more value than anything else that you could ever accomplish in this world.

If you have invited Jesus Christ to come into your life, I would love to hear from you. You can write to me at the following email address...

TheEconomicCollapseBlog @ Hotmail.com

We are entering a period of time that the Bible refers to as the last days. It will be a period of great darkness and the world is going to become increasingly unstable. According to Jesus, there has never been a time like it before, and there will never be a time like it again. But in the middle of all of this, God is going to do great things. He is raising up a Remnant that will keep His commandments, that will boldly proclaim the gospel of salvation through faith in Jesus Christ, and that will see their message confirmed by the power of the Holy Spirit just like the very first believers in Jesus did. This is already happening all over the globe even though no organization is in charge of it. You can read about the Remnant in Revelation 12:17 and Revelation 14:12. God is starting to bring things full circle. The Remnant of the last days is going to do things the way that the Christians of the first century did things. Have you ever wondered why so many Christian churches today do not resemble what you see in the Bible? Well, the sad truth is that over the centuries churches got away from doing the things that the Scriptures tell us to do, but now God is restoring all things. Without God we can do nothing, but with God all things are possible.

Today, we have an even greater opportunity than the first century Christians did in some ways. During the first century, there were only about 200 million people on this planet. Today, there are more than 7 billion. That means that there are about 35 times as many people living on the planet today than there were back then.

The global population has experienced exponential growth over the past couple of centuries, and that means that we have the opportunity to impact more lives than anyone else ever has. I believe that the greatest move of God that the world has ever seen is coming, and I believe that millions upon millions of souls will be brought into the kingdom during the years ahead. I encourage you to be a part of what is happening.

As the global economy collapses and unprecedented troubles break out around the globe, people are going to be looking for answers. Hundreds of millions of people will have their lives totally turned upside down and will be consumed with despair. Instead of giving in to fear like everyone else will be, it will be a great opportunity for the people of God to rise up and take the message of life to a lost and dying world.

Yes, there will be great persecution. The world system absolutely hates the gospel, and the Bible tells us that eventually Christians will be hunted down and killed for what they believe.

But those that have read the end of the book know that we win in the end. The Bible tells us that Jesus is coming back, and He will reign forever and ever. God loves you very much and He wants to make your life a greater adventure than you ever imagined that it possibly could be. Yes, there will be hardships in this world, but if you are willing to pursue God with a passion and become totally sold out for Him, you can make an eternal difference in countless lives.

When you get a chance, go read the book of Acts. Do you want your own life to look like that?

It can.

In these last days, those that have a passion for God and a passion for reaching the lost are going to turn this world upside down with the gospel of Jesus Christ.

The Scriptures tell us that "there is joy in the presence of the angels of God over one sinner that repents." When even a single person makes a commitment to Jesus Christ, there is great celebration in heaven.

As millions upon millions of precious souls are brought into the kingdom in the years ahead, what do you think the atmosphere in heaven is going to look like?

Yes, darkness and evil will also prosper in the days ahead. A one world government, a one world economy and a one world religion are coming. This world system will utterly hate the Remnant and will try to crush us with everything that they have got.

It is going to take great strength and great courage to stand against the world system in the times that are coming. You have the opportunity to be a part of a greater adventure than anything that Hollywood ever dreamed up, and in the end it may cost you your life.

But in Revelation chapter 2, Jesus promises us that if we are "faithful unto death" that He will give us "a crown of life".

For those of us that have a relationship with Jesus, we know that we have the ultimate happy ending. Jesus has forgiven our sins and has given us eternal life, and nobody can ever take that away from us.

Life is like a coin – you can spend it any way that you want, but you can only spend it once.

Spend your life on something that really matters.

God is raising up a Remnant that is going to shake the world, and you do not want to miss out on the great move of God that is coming. It is going to be unlike anything that any of us have ever seen before.

If you enjoyed this book, I encourage you to also connect with me on the Internet. You can find my work at the following websites...

The Economic Collapse Blog:
http://theeconomiccollapseblog.com/

End Of The American Dream:
http://endoftheamericandream.com/

The Most Important News:
http://themostimportantnews.com/

Thank you for taking the time to read this book to the end. I would love to hear any feedback that you may have. Just like the rest of you, I am always learning.

My wife and I are praying for you, and for all of those that will end up reading this book.

May the Lord bless you and keep you.

May the Lord make His face shine upon you and be gracious to you.

May the Lord lift up His countenance upon you and give you His peace.

Michael Snyder – the author of The Rapture Verdict